OPTIONS IN ROMAN CATHOLICISM

AN INTRODUCTION

NATHAN R. KOLLAR
EDITOR

Cover Design
Judith L. Reynolds

ACKNOWLEDGEMENTS

All biblical quotations are taken from The
Jerusalem Bible, copyright c 1966 by Darton,
Longman & Todd, Ltd. and Doubleday and
Company, Inc.
Used by permission of the publisher.

CONTENTS

iii

PREFACE

This book is written by Roman Catholics for those who wish to learn about Roman Catholicism. The best way to learn about a Roman Catholic's religion is to ask. This is what I did. I asked some members of the College Theology Society what they wanted in an introductory text for college students. They offered suggestions. I then asked experienced teachers, who were also Catholics, to write chapters dealing with the topics suggested by the members of the Society. Options is the result.

This book is not an ordinary introductory text. It describes the diversity in Roman Catholicism. Controversy and diversity are seldom part of an introductory text. Usually the arguments among the authorities and the leaders in a field of study are left for graduate school. Introductory texts ordinarily give one point of view clearly and simply so the beginner has the tools to continue thinking and working in the field. This is not so in Options because we take for granted the college student has thought about religion many times in the past. The student is not a novice in reflecting on the religious dimension of life, even though the student may lack the precise vocabulary and ability to articulate that reflection. Each author in Options provides the reader with the tools to think and work in the academic discipline of Roman Catholic studies. At the same time, however, each author admits a complex diversity of interpretation and living within Roman Catholicism.

This diversity is the first and most important lesson to be learned about Roman Catholics: we are not the same in culture, education, economic status, articulation of doctrinal standards or moral ideas. Such a claim may seem too strong to many readers. They might easily respond that this claim is simplice, too bold, or absolutely wrong. Such responses lead to the second lesson.

The second lesson to be learned about Roman Catholics is that we argue about how to express, celebrate and live our way of life. The chapters of this book will beget some of the same responses as did my statement about diversity. The chapters will seem too simple to some readers, too complicated to others, too absolute to some, not absolute enough to still others.

Such responses to the chapters indicate that the students, as well as the teachers, are part of the pluralism in the Church. They have been thinking about these topics. They have formulated opinions about them. Indeed many have taken options in religious living. This text will challenge these options by showing there are other choices and by demanding that the options already taken be discussed at a college level.

To aid such discussion and clarification of individual options, each chapter is designed to initiate the involvement of the student, instructor, and those outside the classroom. Learning happens beyond the written text. Each chapter facilitates that learning by situating the topic in everyday life, discussing the complexity of the issue and then presenting some of the options or choices available to the contemporary Catholic. Finally, each chapter ends with a series of questions for personal reflection, group discussion, and content selection. These questions are essential to understanding the chapter. If taken seriously, they challenge the student to deal with this way of life as more than a mental exercise. A religion, if studied seriously, challenges our present way of living. This text does this.

The study of religion is a serious exercise. It must be serious because it deals with the basic questions of life and existence. The third lesson to be learned about Roman Catholics is that we take our religion seriously. There seems to be a common desire among Catholics to have one faith: one definite articulation, celebration and living of our religion. There are many historical reasons for this desire, but I think there is a deeper, metaphysical reason for such desire: each person is unique, yet incomplete. We are a question waiting for an answer; pieces of a puzzle waiting to be whole; a story waiting to be told; a desire waiting to be fulfilled. We are, as these images of our incompleteness make so clear, a mystery. In our mystery of incompleteness, we tend to claim completion before the proper time. An answer becomes the answer; this picture becomes the picture; this story, the story and this fulfillment, the fulfillment. In other words, by our very nature we want to be complete, but also by our very nature we will never be complete in the world as we know it. The Catholic tends to become too serious about this particular expression of the answer to life's question. Because we do take our questions and life's answer(s) seriously, there is a constant tension between my answer or faith, your answer (faith), and our answer (faith). One purpose of this text is to clarify the tension, allow for healthy options within this tension, and invite an increase of options within the mystery of that communal quest for life's answer which is the Roman Catholic church.

Chapter One asks how we became American Roman Catholics. A complete answer to the question takes volumes. We have selected a few significant "pasts" to demonstrate the diversity of the past and possible reasons for tensions in the present. The chapter does not have to be read all at once. Parts of it can be read while investigating the themes of the other chapters.

Chapter Two seeks to find God in our Christian life. We find that God is present in many events and speaks in many ways, but is especially present in bible and people.

When we realize the presence of God, how do we respond individually and communally? Chapter Three deals with our response in faith and belief.

Chapters Four and Five treat our response in daily living. The goals and responsibilities which are consequent upon God's revelation are investigated. What is a good person? If God is present, revealing an answer to our question of life, we must respond by living a life worthy of both question and answer. These chapters show us our choices.

We do not seek answers alone. We do not walk the way of life alone. We share a past, present and future with those who share a common belief, celebration, ethical stance and spirit. Chapters Six and Seven look more deeply into our life together - the Church. Who are we? How do we help each other to become what we ought to be?

Chapter Eight reflects upon the experiences of those who have worshipped in order to help them understand their experiences. It demonstrates the ways and significance of celebrating who we are.

Finally, in Chapter Nine, the student is asked to review his or her options. To discuss and think of options without facing one's own choices is a mental exercise lacking seriousness. A serious and sincere investigation requires that the reader think about the available options, examine the ones taken in the past and decide to live in the light of them or make new ones. Chapter Nine helps one to choose life-giving options.

These chapters and this book are not finished. What began as a question to some members of the College Theology Society is a question to each reader and instructor who uses this book. What should be included in an introductory text about American Roman Catholicism? What can we do better than what we have done in these chapters? These questions are yours as well as the authors of these chapters. If you answer them, and send them to me, the editor, we can continue to develop a worthwhile text.

There are many individuals who have answered these questions and helped develop the text so far: the students of St. John Fisher College and the University of Rochester who attended my Options courses over the last seven years; the students at Quincy College, Ill., Catholic University and the University of California at Fullerton who have helped the other authors test their ideas; Dr. William Sullivan, a colleague at St. John Fisher, who risked another Introductory Course both to test and critique the manuscript; Fr. Joseph Hart of St. Bernard's Institute who labored

over many of these chapters in the midst of his own
writing; Dr. Christine Bochen, who took time from her
already too busy schedule to read and critique the
manuscript; and finally to my family, especially my
wife Judy, who gave me the option to spend many hours
to finish this text. To all of these a sincere thanks.
To those of you who read this, here is an invitation
to add your name to the above list..

Nathan R. Kollar
July 4, 1982
St. John Fisher College
Rochester, New York
14618

x

INTRODUCTION

Senior year of high school is a time of reflection and of joy. Reflection on what to do with one's life; joy, that a significant preparatory period is at an end. Choices are made as a consequence of both reflection and joy. One chooses to go to college or to enter full time into the work force. Either of these choices affects the rest of the graduate's life. Yet the option for full time employment or college is not the result of one single choice or action at the end of the senior year. No. Many choices made by oneself or others contributes to this very significant option of life after high school. One's choice of being a Roman Catholic is also a significant choice in life. It too includes many other choices. As a life-choice it shares the characteristics of all other life-choices.

When we concentrate on one choice, it is easy to forget what has already been chosen. To choose a college education, for instance, means that in the past our parents chose to place us in circumstances conducive to learning to read, to write, to learn mathematics. Without their choices our present choice would be meaningless since we would not be able to make it. We also made many choices before the one to go to college: to spend time studying, to sacrifice some favorite amusement in order to study for an exam, to associate with those in school who shared our interests. Some of these choices were easy; some, more difficult. But we made them and as a consequence chose to continue our schooling. There are always many options completed before we face an individual option, and once making one option the way is open to make more. Following the option or way of Roman Catholicism means we have already taken many footsteps upon this path. Each step is an option. It is true, too, that we may stand on a particular part of the path and not realize how far we have walked, our past; or, in what direction we are going, our future. The truth of the matter is that we do not stand anywhere within Catholicism alone. We are not a Catholic individually but share a past and future with others.

Where we stand on the way of Roman Catholicism is the
result of the choices of others as well as our own.
To choose well, we must be sensitive to our own past,
present, and future options as well as those with
whom we share the Catholic way of life. This book
will suggest ways of being sensitive to those many
factors which enter into our choosing to remain Roman
Catholic.

     To even suggest that there are options or choices
in Roman Catholicism may seem strange. The Roman
Catholic Church in the United States has been portrayed
both by many of its people and by the media as a
church of rigid uniformity. Those who have done and
are doing the portraying do not realize how diverse
we are. This book will demonstrate this diversity.
The uniformity of the Church in the United States is
a stereotype contrary to the reality of a church of
many customs, ideas, ideals, arguments and struggles.
Our hope is that the reader will see this variety of
options.

I. AMERICAN CATHOLICISM: SHARING A PAST: OPTIONS IN HISTORY

NATHAN KOLLAR

Two Catholics

As Joseph walked up the aisle to communion, he was apprehensive and confused. Everything was different. This Mass at college - his first - wasn't like any Catholic Mass he'd been to before. As he approached the altar he realized that there were three students behind the priest holding the chalice. "They expect me to drink the wine!" he thought. Nervously, he opened his mouth. The priest paused, glanced at Joseph's folded hands, and placed the host on his tongue. Joseph quickly blessed himself and went to his seat to kneel down only to remember, too late, that there were no kneelers in this chapel.

***

As Ann walked from the priest's house, she felt it was spring. She had just celebrated the sacrament of reconciliation. She had returned to the Catholic Church.

Ann was 36 years old. Fifteen years ago she stopped going to church. She didn't stop because she disliked it; rather, it just didn't seem attractive anymore. Like an old bike lying abandoned in the attic, she left the Church unattended, unused and forgotten. Fifteen years passed, and she suddenly realized that she was curious about what happened to her church. An advertisement for an adult-education course caught her eye. She attended the class and discovered a church full of diversity and enthusiasm.

A Common Problem

Joseph and Ann are faced with a similar difficulty: how to live as a Catholic in a Church that

1

challenges us with a diversity of options. Ann, in returning to the Catholic way of life after 15 years, must find her way. Her problem is "how." Joseph, in encountering a different style of Catholicism on campus, must find the best way to live his Catholicism. His problem too, is "how."

This book introduces us to the various ways a person can be a Catholic -- the "how" which Ann and Joseph must face. Yet part of every "how" is "why." Why do we do what we do? Why do Catholics celebrate Mass, favor certain ethical positions, or call their religious leaders Father, Bishop, or Pope? One way of answering the how's and why's that are part of every Catholic's life is to look to the past. In seeing and understanding the past which all Catholics share, we can begin to understand the "why" of the present and the "how" of acting in the future.

Catholic Pasts

Some of us, when we look at our own or another's past, concentrate on how much we have remained the same over the years; others look and are amazed at the change which has occurred. These are two common methods for interpreting the past, including the Church's past. We tend to emphasize one or the other of these attitudes in reflecting upon life. Some people feel the most significant dimension of life is that which remains stable and doesn't change; others feel the important part is how they and society change and adapt.

The Church participates in both these dimensions: some aspects of it remain the same; others change. Those symbols, systems of symbols, and symbolic actions which constitute the Church are to the Church's life as Ann's words, actions, and patterns of behavior are to Ann. When we look for sameness or change in the Church we must look for these as they occur among humans, not machines. We look for organic change. Identity or change in the Church, over time, is not similar to a stamped machine part, but to that of a growing human being.

2

When we look at Ann, for instance, we hear words and see actions which make her a person. The way she speaks and acts changes as she acts and reacts to life. She may use the same words but say them differently; employ the same mannerisms yet use them more effectively as she ages. Anyone who has lived with her for 36 years may not recognize the change. Someone who has not seen her in 16 years, however, would be amazed at how she looks, talks, acts and dresses. That's because Ann, like other human beings, can grow and change while remaining the same. A child of five and the same person at 95 are the same, yet there has been change over the 90 years. Human "sameness" is not the "sameness" of things.

The same type of change and continuity found among people through time is present in the Church. When Ann returned to it, for instance, she experienced the Mass in English, saw the priest's face during Mass rather than his back, and was able to understand what he said and did. This was quite different from what she experienced in the past. Yet there were words and actions which were the same: bread, wine, kneeling, sitting, reading, praying, singing, and much more. These symbols were there 16 years ago, but because the context had changed, Ann experienced differently. Just as there is something the same about Ann over time, so there is something the same about the Church over time. These "same things" are difficult to enumerate. Just as one person focuses on one dimension of Ann -- her face; another person on something else -- her personality, in the same way, each of us looks to one or another dimension of the Church for a claim to sameness or difference. No two people see the Church in exactly the same way, but they do see some same things. We will call these same things the constitutive elements. They are experienced differently at different times by each person. There is not complete agreement as to what all of these constitutive elements are.

What we are about to do is look at the Church of the past with the purpose of seeing some of these constitutive elements in various contexts. We will go back in time to understand some of the past options

3

present in today's church. We go back to the past as Ann and Joseph reflect upon their future: from the present. Ann returned, for instance, to the Church with her present problems, not with the ones she had 16 years ago, although these, too, helped shape her. In the same way we go back to our past from the present. It is our present concerns which shape the questions which we ask of the history we share with fellow Catholics.

These present concerns determine the four pasts we examine: how we began; how we establish our present institutional forms and dominant symbols; how we changed our view of the world, and how we became part of the American way of life. These pasts are with us as individuals and institution. We cannot escape these pasts. To be identified as Roman Catholic is to be identified with the pasts of Roman Catholicism. An understanding of these four pasts will help us understand the present tensions in Catholic life. Class discussion, lectures, and personal investigation will deepen this understanding and help decide where we think we fit in.

THE PAST AS BEGINNING 33-450 A.D.

In every beginning there is both old and new, but in a beginning the new overshadows the old. Beginnings determine the direction of a group of people or an individual. Christianity has had many beginnings. Three significant ones are among the Jews, among the people of the Mediterranean, and within the Roman Empire of Constantine.

Three Beginnings

The first Christians were Palestinian Jews. Only a handful among the thousands of Jews were Christian. As Jews, they followed the Jewish laws, customs, language, holy books and prejudices. The non-Jews, or Gentiles, regarded them as Jews, not Christians. These Jewish Christians were different from other Jews, however, because they believed that Jesus was the beginning of God's reign and that they were his

followers. This belief and their dedication was a
beginning.

These Jewish Christians told other Jews and Gentiles about Jesus. In the telling, they recounted
what he had done and said in such a way that the
listener could understand who he was. They spoke of
resurrection because people were concerned about death.
They tried to live a life of love and speak of their
oneness in Jesus because people felt the divisions
between themselves. As a result of this teaching and
example, both Jews and Gentiles wished to become
Christian. But the problem for the early Christians
was whether the Gentiles had to become Jews in order
to be Christian. Did the Gentiles have to follow the
same Jewish laws they followed? In particular, both
Jewish Christians and Gentile Christians were faced
with the difficulty of the Jewish obligation to male
circumcision. The Christians thought, argued, and
prayed over the problem. They decided in the words of
an early document (Acts 15:29), "It has been decided
by the Holy Spirit and by ourselves not to saddle you
with any burden beyond these essentials: you are to
abstain from food sacrificed to idols, from blood,
from the meat of strangled animals, and from fornica-
tion. Avoid these, and you will do what is right."
These words portray a rejection and an acceptance of
the Christians' Jewish past. When they refused to
attend the circus, gladiatorial combats, or sacrificial banquets, they rejected their Gentile past. The
newness of their beginning left them isolated from
their past whether they were Jew or Gentile. They
were misfits, nonconformists.

This status of nonconformist changed in 313 A.D.,
when the Edict of Milan accorded Christians full
legal status with the pagan cults. This meant that
the Roman Empire no longer persecuted Christians but
recognized them as a legal religion. They were given
large buildings for their use and people flocked to
become members. The world of the Empire began to
become the world of the Church. The challenge was what
to do with this new-found success. The Church accepted
the influx of new members as well as the social
responsibility for the exercise of authority in this

5

situation. The Church accepted and formalized the way of organization, worship, and belief of its immediate past, and rejected the idea that the small-community atmosphere and opposition to the state which characterized it up until 313 was essential to Christianity. Between 313 and 450 the Church expanded and built a way of life which continues to influence every Christian Church.

Organization

The Church's style of living evolved from the people who were Christians. The forms of organization and attitudes of leadership of Jewish, Greek, and Roman Christians became part of Christian living. The only exception was that the style of organizational life had to reflect the characteristics of love and service which were inherent to the Christian way of life.

As a small, persecuted group, the early Christians had a feeling of togetherness, self-sacrifice, and mutual forebearance characteristic of minority groups. The Apostles, those who witnessed the resurrected Jesus, could be heard and seen. The Christians' sense of Jesus within the community was tangible in every meeting and breaking of bread. They were brothers and sisters to each other.

In the beginning the style of leadership was diverse, with each Christian community developing a way of living which fit its unique needs. Some communities were led by a group of people similar to a board of directors of a school or corporation; others were led by one person who spoke in God's name.

As Gentile Christianity grew, and the pressure of Christian arguments and divisions increased, the dominant style of leadership began to focus on one person as the leader of the community, the monarchical bishop. He was selected by the Christian community for the Christian community. Once selected, he, together with his brother priests and deacons, showed by word and example how the Christian life was to be lived.

As the Church developed after 313, it accepted
the forms of organization of the Roman empire. The
geographical division of towns, Roman Law, and
methods of bureaucracy became the Church's dioceses,
law, and processes of recourse and judgment. But now
the law, bureaucracy and judgment were to be in the
service of love.

In each of these three beginnings, the way the
Church organized itself, selected its leaders, discovered the way of the gospels, and worshipped reflected its past, its belief in Jesus, and its present
culture.

Worship

Synagogue and daily prayer were the core of early
Christian worship. As the Christians began to separate
themselves from the Jews, the influence of this first
beginning shaped their worship. Judaism influenced
early Christian worship much more than the culture of
Rome and Greece. Sunday, the day of Resurrection,
became the focus of Christian gathering. The Christian
assembly ritual was a union of the Jewish synagogue
services of readings, sermons, and prayers and the
shared meal in Jesus' memory. Jesus was present in
the reading, remembering, eating, and drinking.

Christians also prayed six times a day as every
pious Jew did: at daybreak, before going to sleep,
and at midnight, as well as the third, sixth, and
ninth hour after rising. Daily prayer and Sunday
assembly were essential to the Christian life.

As the Christian community grew it adapted. By
345 an increased membership resulted in crowded litur-
gies. Sunday Eucharist took on the air of a celebration, and large groups of people and enormous churches
resulted in processions, prayers, and ceremonies adapted to church life from civil life. Gone were the
intimate Eucharists of persecuted Christians, the
stricter demands of baptism, the thrill of being different from others. The Church moved into the cathe-
dral and the established way of life.

7

Belief and Doctrine

The early Christians believed that the reign of God began in Jesus, was present in His Spirit, and would be fulfilled at the end of time. God's reign was extended by the recognition that Jesus was the one, true sovereign. It was expressed wherever the genuine need of others was fulfilled. To cry "Jesus is Lord" was to express His role in the world's salvation which was to overcome the powers of evil in this world.

To shout the conviction that "Jesus is Lord" and explain that conviction to Jew and Gentile are two distinct actions. Gradually this first shout evolved to a communal declaration called the Apostles' Creed.

The statements in the Apostles' Creed reflect the many controversies in the early Church about Jesus, His Father, His birth, and His Spirit in the Church. A declaration that God was Father and Creator of heaven and earth may seem a truism to us. But to those early Christians it proclaimed the evils of Gnosticism which claimed that the material things of this world were evil and that the creator of the earth was the devil, not the Father of Jesus. The Church rejected these ideas.

Such challenges to and arguments about doctrine arose as Christians thought about their faith and tried to live it. Beginning with the Council of Nicae in 325, the arguments became formalized in the ecumenical councils. These councils were assemblies of bishops and other ecclesiastical representatives of the Church brought together to solve the significant problems of the time. One of the dominant problems of belief was whether Jesus was God. Scripture and custom were not precise about Jesus' total relationship to His Father. As a consequence, people began to argue about who Jesus was. The Nicene Creed (381) said on Sunday is the Church's official statement about Jesus.

Discussions about belief always occur with the assumptions and the ways of argument of the era. If, for instance, the way of arguing and coming to the truth

for a culture is to hear the revelation of the Spirit
as voiced by a member of the community, then the people
of that time will search for a person who will speak
in such a way. This is what happened in the arguments
with the Gnostics. The Apostles and their successors
were looked to as special sources of knowledge about
the faith, and were seen to speak in the Spirit's
name. As a consequence, the Apostolic Sees and the
Bishops of Jerusalem, Antioch, and Rome gained special
importance in the Church.

Since the Christian scriptures were already
written and recognized as part of Christian life, the
community looked to these foundational books to aid
them in their faith and doctrine. In the arguments
about the nature of Jesus in 325, the Christians
searched the scriptures for some hint as to whether
Jesus is God, man, or both. Some of those arguing
about Jesus' relationship to the Father were knowl-
edgeable in the philosophy of the times. Their learning shaped the Church's vision of Jesus. Scripture,
reason, experience, and authority have always had a
place in formulating Christian belief. Sometimes one
of these sources of knowledge rather than another
determines the direction of the argument. Today we are
millions of volumes and millions of people away from
the first statements of belief, but we use these same
instruments for dealing with understanding the faith.

End

Every beginning ends. By 450 the peace of Rome
gave way to warring northern European tribes, and the
Graeco-Roman culture which first rejected and then
accepted Christianity came to an end. Christians saw
the destruction of their world: their churches,
society, cities, and way of life. Northern Europeans
now dominated the Mediterranean, not by Roman Law but
by powerful armies. Christians were faced with an end
and, possibly, a new beginning. Many contemporary
Christians look to the time before 450 as the past which
fits our present future.

If people are fortunate enough to live to old age,
they can look back to a period of their life when it
was established, to a time when they lived in one house,
stayed at one job, made a place for themselves in their
neighborhood, and helped the children grow to adult-
hood. Being established for an individual or a group
is a time of deepening, of increasing control, of
exuberance and curiosity, of feeling whole. The
Church was established from 1073, the time of the
reform Pope Gregory VII, to 1517, the moment when
Martin Luther, the Augustinian priest, posted his
theses on the door of the castle Church of Wittenberg.
During this time, the Church was the basis of all life
in Medieval Europe. Thought, philosophy, science,
administration of justice, education, charitable
activity, and work were all done within the framework
of a Christian culture. Life was inconceivable without the Christian way of life as lived by the people
and interpreted by popes, bishops, and theologians.

The people understood the universe to be a series
of inter-dependent parts from the lowest, the inani-
mate, to the highest, God. Life was a ladder of ani-
mate being where there was a place for everyone and
everyone had a place. If all these component beings
did what they were supposed to do, the whole universe
functioned properly. God called each person, animal,
and thing to perform a specific task in this hierarchy.
To fulfill this task brought the rewards of heaven.
God created this society as well as the entire universe. God was seen as guiding the decrees of Church
and secular officials.

Feudalism

This organic hierarchy had a social structure:
Feudalism. Feudalism was a replacement of law and
money by obligation and tithe. These obligations and
tithes permeated one's whole life so that loyalty was
the dominant virtue. Life was judged by one's loyalty
to God, to one's Lord (Baron), to one's love.

This emphasis upon loyalty was different from our

10

present acceptance of freedom and love as important virtues. One of the most important differences was that one's position in this feudal society was based on status, not individual initiative. A person's place in society was set by birth. Once established it could not be lost, nor another gained: once a shoemaker, always a shoemaker, or a miller, or a smith.

Society was divided into the noble and the peasant or servile class. War, sport, and high adventure were the noble's lifestyle; work and service were the lot of the peasant. The clergy and religious belonged to either the noble or servile class, depending upon their birth. Except for the noble, his family, the parish priest, and a few administrative officials, the entire population of a large manor consisted of persons of servile class. Our type of middle class did not exist.

Private property was suspect. The reason for work, property, and exchange of goods was to help people get to heaven. No person, it was preached, should expend energy to pursue luxury, to be comfortable. Taking interest on loans (usury) was condemned and goods were to be sold for a just price. Profit for profit's sake was avarice, which was one of the most dangerous of sins.

This feudal-pyramid structure, a ladder-like conception of the universe, was reflected in the way Christians viewed their relationship with God. At the top was God the Father and His son Jesus. Then, in order, Mary, the Saints, the Pope, the Bishops and nobles, the priests and monks, and the people. Christians believed that the power of God came through these intermediaries as water through a pipe. People would not think of going directly to God for anything. Instead, they would ask higher intermediaries in this chain of being to intervene with God on their behalf. In a like manner, people would not think of going directly to the Lord of the Manor with a request. They went through proper channels for the materials for physical or spiritual life. Loyalty was shown by recognizing one's interdependence in all things.

11

The liturgy expressed this world view. It was different from today. Since only ten percent of the population could read and write, the liturgy could not be celebrated as it is with an educated laity and clergy. Nor could the strong feeling of communal life and concern be present, as in the fourth century, because the Mass was in Latin, not in the people's language. The focus of the Mass was upon the priest making Christ -- the all powerful -- present in the bread, which by now had become a circular white wafer, the host. The Mass was the priest's work. He said it by himself, in Latin, in a low voice with his back to the people. Bells rang to call the people to see when the bread was elevated. The people believed that seeing this bread was a privilege and a source of power and favor. This desire of the people to see the host, called "communion of the eyes," caused the priest to pause during the Eucharistic prayer to show the host to them by holding it above his head. The elevation of the bread and the chalice in the following centuries originated in this liturgical practice of "communion of the eyes." Modification of other liturgical practices followed the pattern found in the Mass. There was a shift of emphasis from community participation to individual salvation; from celebration of the community to the power of the priest; from the quality of the liturgical act to the quantity of liturgical actions. This shift which occurred in the Middle Ages was present in the Church until the reforms of Vatican II (1962-65).

The sacraments, however, were not the core of the people's lives. Relics, devotion to the saints, and indulgences were the touchstones of their spirituality, their life with God. Saints were prayed to for better health, for finding lost articles, for an increase in crops, for winning wars. A saint could be found to help any earthly activity. The relics were the bones, hair, clothes or any other article pertaining to the saint. These relics were believed to be a source of power, a place where God acted in a special way. People wanted these relics because, from their perspective, the relics controlled the actions of God upon the earth. The relics, along with the holy people, places, and times were a source of miracles

12

-- ways God would break into the ordinary world of the Christians and do wondrous deeds. Even the Eucharistic bread was used as a source of miracles. People would take it and place it at the corner of their home to keep the evil spirits away.

God was the source of miracles and of power. He was the all-powerful being who lived beyond the world but directly influenced it through his intermediaries. God was the supreme ruler who could make the rain fall or make a person die. If God's laws were broken, Christians felt they would pay the consequences through suffering and death. If God was honored, they could look forward to a life of reward and influence.

The Church was the bridge to God. Between God in his heaven and humans on this earth stood the Church, the bridge between the natural and supernatural worlds. The natural world was what was seen and touched. It was the world filled with sin, flesh, limitation, and ignorance. The supernatural world was the world of God, perfection, the spirit, unlimited abilities, and the dominance of the mind. The Church brought the world of God into the world of humans and the world of humans into the world of God.

The Church, through the papacy and the monasteries, established this society and, in turn, was formed by it. Let us take each of these in turn.

The Pope was the apex of medieval social life. Innocent III said it best in 1198:

Only St. Peter was invested with the plenitude of power. See then what manner of servant this is, appointed over God's household; he is the vicar of Jesus Christ, the successor of Peter, the Lord's anointed...set in the midst between man and God...less than God but greater than man, judge of all men and judged by none. (Selected Letters Concerning England C. R. Cheney & W. H. Semple, eds. p. x.)

By the time of Innocent the III (1198-1216), the Bishop of Rome was the Noble Lord of large areas of Italy and Southern France, the center of a bureaucracy which was the ultimate court of appeal of all Bishops. And the Pope was elected by a select group of Cardinals rather than the people of Rome. In other words, the pope and his assistants, the curia, had centralized the administration of the Church so that what Innocent III claimed as true in theory was true in fact. Because the pope was central to the life of the Middle Ages, his attitude and the attitude of his administrative bureaus were essential to the life of this time. There was much fraud, bribery, licentiousness, and splendor in the court of the pope. In fact, all external criteria indicated that the center of this established Church looked more to this earth for its livelihood rather than to heaven.

Monasticism

Monastic life was the ideal of this era. Everyone in the monastery had a place and there was a place for everyone. Work, prayer, and personal relationships were carried out for and in the love of God. To understand monastic life one must understand its origins. Initially, monasticism was a radical response to the Church's success. When the Church was legalized in 313 it began to expand. Some Christians felt that such a success and expansion were bad because it was destructive of the spirit of self-sacrifice and martyrdom which formed the early Church. These individuals looked for a way to continue the enthusiasm, camaraderie, and feelings of self-discipline which were present in that early Church. The lifestyle which resulted from this desire grew into monastic life. This way of life sought a simple style of living rather than the glamor and sensuality of court life; it focused on an otherworldly life of the spirit in contrast to that of marriage and family; it offered the dedication of one's will to another as an example of how everyone should give themselves to the will of the Father. This lifestyle and the monasteries which grew up to house it were responsible for the survival of Western culture during the early Middle Ages. Dedicated to the love of God, these men and women preserved the loves of earth by establishing centers of education, copying books, and creating new agricultural techniques and technological inventions. The successful Church they rejected at one time became a Church whose success they insured at another. The consequence of their success offered the Middle Ages a proven way of life and happiness. The vows of poverty, chastity, and obedience were seen as the ideal for both layperson and clergy. The norm of holiness was the monastic life.

If Medieval society was to survive, these two pillars, pope and monastery, had to live their ideals. The story of the collapse of the established Church and the society it helped create is the story of attempts to reform the Church in head (Pope) and members (especially the monasteries) so that the society itself would reflect in fact what it proclaimed in ideal.

The ideal was that society was united through love and interdependence. The fact was that this society was torn by rising nationalism and aggresive capitalism. The ideal presented a society with a pope who stood between God and people, ruling in charity and harmony. The fact was there had been three popes at the same time (1378-1417), that offices and sacraments were bought and sold, that the pope and his curia stood with hands outstretched for money. The ideal was that the priests and religious were learned and dedicated to the service of the people and God. The fact was that many of them were ignorant, with their only function to say Mass or read the breviary, their prayer book. The ideal was that the religious and priests were to be poor and celibate, but the fact was that many sought increased wealth and were either married or had a concubine. The Established Church needed to change because the ideals it presented were not found reflected in the daily life of most of the people. On October 31, 1517 a 34-year-old Augustinian friar, Father Martin Luther, posted 95 theses in Latin on the door of a church in Wittenberg. This was a traditional way of challenging to debate one's academic colleagues. This act, unforseen by Luther, marked the beginning of the Protestant reformation, a period which dramatically changed the relationship between the Established Church and society.

Once Luther challenged the Established Church it would never again be the same. This past, described as the time of establishment, is a past still idealized by many Roman Catholics. The theology, spirituality, liturgy, and economic life are looked to as models for the future. This is a past honored by some as the way of Roman Catholic life.

THE PAST AS CHANGE

When raindrops fall from the sky, it is difficult to watch them change positions. All we know is that we are wet. When a tree grows, we see the changes over seasons, not minutes. When a candle is lit, the room becomes light but we don't experience the movement of the light. Change is sometimes readily apparent, sometimes not. Historical change is similar to the change we see around us. Sometimes it's quick, sometimes slow. Sometimes it builds up for a long while so that we sense its coming; other times it breaks upon us suddenly and without warning.

The historical change we are about to describe encompasses hundreds, some would claim thousands, of years. We are going to look briefly at two significant pasts: the classical or pre-modern age, and the modern. Today we live in the post-modern age, a time whose history has yet to be written. To understand the Church and the development of her doctrine, worship,aand organization, we must become sensitive to significant social and intellectual changes which occurred in these eras.

The turning point is 1648 and the signing of the Treaty of Westphalia. This treaty between Germany, France, and other nations concluded that the affairs of state could no longer be discussed or conducted on a religious basis, and laid the groundwork for the accommodation to ecclesiastical pluralism. Religious indifference was both a cause and a result of the treaty. The treaty put into political terms what had already begun in the previous century: a transition

from viewing the world in absolute, changeless, un-
related terms to seeing everything as temporal, relative and changing. But this is getting ahead of ourselves in the description of change. Let us first
look at significant social change.

Social Change

The rise of cities and the subsequent trend
toward industrialization was the source of that change
called modernization. As life became more urbanized
and, later, the Industrial Revolution took hold,
significant changes occurred not only in the milieu of
people's lives but also in the shape of their problems
and their thought processes. Five of the most significant changes which influenced religious life are:

1. Change in the way goods were produced and
distributed. As population, buying power, and demand
increased, goods began to be mass produced and distributed over wide areas. Mass production meant that
workers became more separate from what they produced.
For instance, a worker might be responsible for only
one part of a machine, not for the entire product.
In the extreme they were viewed as slightly different
from the machines they used. They were given little
or no freedom in deciding when and where to work.
Because of this, people began to be seen more in terms
of what they did as a worker than who they were as
people.

2. Change in the ability and use of machines.
An almost total transition to the use of machines
and mechanical power made the machine itself become
the model of perfection. The human body began to be
described as composed of certain parts which were put
together to produce a human. The machine, capable of
producing identical products, became the image of
sameness as well as change. People began to think
that a human, to be perfect, must be able to act like
a machine -- do the same thing, in the same way, time
after time. As scientific understanding increased,
nature lost its centrality and God who was seen as
controlling natural phenomena was challenged. The
destruction of the mystery of nature led to the absence

17

of the mystery of God. God began to be imagined as a
machine rather than a person. Machines, not humans,
were the best regulators of life; a God which resem-
bled a machine was more easily understood than one
that was not.

     3. <u>Change in the place of work and life</u>. As the
population became increasingly urbanized, traditional
controls and loyalties broke down. In 1850 only four
cities had a population of a million or more; by 1960
there were 141. The earth's urban population was
doubling every eleven years. Workers changed homes
and jobs more easily, and, as a consequence, the family
rather than the job became the place where affection
was deserved and expected. As family, work, religion,
play, entertainment became more separate, life became
increasingly secularized. Doing something because
of social pressures -- the usual way in an agricultural
society -- was looked down upon. Some psychiatrists
have even described such pressures as unhealthy, since
their theory of psychological maturity reflected the
importance of the disjointed life of the modern person.
These changes meant that the Church began to be seen
as a voluntary organization where one cared for one's
spiritual life.

     The decrease of such communal controls, high
mobility, and the continuous change in environment and
techniques challenged the ancient idea of commitment
and loyalty to one person and one job. Continuous
change challenged the way of life dependent upon non-
change. Relativity, pluralism, change were seen as
good. Stability, uniformity, and inability to change
and keep up with the times were seen as bad. A person
could not live in the modern world without being able
to deal with change. A religion which argued against
change in a society where change was interpreted as
progress was seen to prevent the individual from dealing with the modern world. Many sociologists considered Roman Catholicism to be such a religion.

     4. <u>Change in the person's control of time</u>.
With the proliferation of accurate time pieces, the
individual became subordinated to the clock. Mechanical time began to dominate daily living and all human

relationships. Mechanical time controlled appointments and the coordination of mechanical and human movements. A worship which included special times, special places, and special people as part of its celebration now had to fit into a way of life which placed importance on uniformity: time was the same, equal, measured in micro-seconds. What we became was more important than what we were. Time measured our pace of becoming.

5. Change in the number and accuracy of the recorded word. With modernization came an increased commitment to records and the conformity to their use for the verification of actions, contacts, and pledges. The widespread use of the printing press after the 15th century increased the written word. Before 1500, Europe produced about a thousand books a year. By 1960 at least one thousand books were produced worldwide each day. Words and information were seen differently after the widespread use of the printing press. The exactness of thoughts and ideas were expressed in these words. The making of contracts was essential for life. Word of mouth and promises were secondary to the written word. Exactness was demanded of all official documents. For a document to be worthwhile, it must be exact. It must reflect clearly one idea, one thought, one truth. Such an idea of life and documentation looked to the Bible with expectations of exactness which the writers of those books were not able to live up to since they came from a world that existed before proliferation of the written word.

Modernization, which was the result of these five changes, left us with a work ethic where personal worth was based on one's capacity to work and ability to earn. This was different from the medieval society where worth was based upon heredity, ordination, or both. Modernization left us more isolated from each other in cities and suburbs rather than close to each other physically and spiritually. Modernization gives us more personal and job freedom. It increased life expectancy, resulting in an ever-expanding population. This growing population, in turn, became more materialistic. People wanted more things and the acquisition of goods became the way to judge the value of an individual. Finally, modernization shook the

foundations of the traditional sources of authority
for truth and morality. The family, the priesthood,
and ancient books were no longer considered to be
sacred and unable to be challenged. Instead, reason
predominated. If tradition could not be proven to
be reasonable, it was abandoned. If tradition could
not be formulated into law, it was abandoned.

The fundamental question is whether these past
changes are of such magnitude as to claim a radical
modification of human life -- a modification similar
to a discovery of a sixth sense. Have these changes
in material things affected the very make-up of the
human person? Have we, as the theologian Bultmann
says, by the invention of the lightbulb changed ourselves in such a significant way so that everything
which occurred in the pre-modern period is radically
different from what happened in the modern? How
different was each era from the other? Which past,
pre-modern or modern, will shape our future?

Some readers might suggest that to change one's
external environment is not to change the individual:
that there is little difference between these pasts.
This may be true. But what if one's internal environment of space, time and value changed? What if individuals began to value events and people in a significantly different way from before? What if they understood their very selves different than before? What
if their basic understanding of truth changed? A
contrast between the pre-modern and the modern age
suggests that this has occurred. Basically, people
came to value becoming and change over being and
stability. To elaborate on this contrast I will first
discuss the pre-modern classical view and then the
modern one.

Classical View

The classical view sees the world as one. Plurality is a curse, if not an impossibility. The laws and
structure of society are the deposit of the prudence
and wisdom of humanity. One cannot change society at
will. There are values which are important and which
have remained important throughout time. These are

the values which should guide us now. People may
differ about what these values are, but the fact is
that there is a hierarchy of values upon which we
can and must base our life. Not only are there values,
laws, and structures which we can know and which are
consistent throughout time, but there is one way of
knowing these permanent dimensions of life. There is
a perennial philosophy which gives us the means to
know and to know well what are the guiding principles
and norms for living. When we know these principles
they are normative for us. True culture is where true
norms are present; here is the true way of life and
knowledge. Barbarians do not recognize the truth.
All people must and should be made to find that which
is best. Education is a way to find the best. Education presents models to be imitated, eternal truths
to be learned, universally valid laws to direct our
life. If we do this our life will have stability,
purpose, immutability, and, as a consequence, immortal-
ity.

Modern View

The modern view is the opposite to the classical
in many ways. The world is not one. There are many
cultures, many meanings, many ways of doing and thinking. All of these are equal. The laws and structures
of society are the result of human will power and
acceptance. These laws and structures may be changed
whenever we want, whenever they are seen as evil.
The facts are what count. These facts can be known
by the scientific method. Truth is what we see, feel,
touch, and know directly, clearly, and with precision.
All else is opinion. Value is subjective. The facts
are objective and capable of being known. We must
always distinguish between what we know and what we
feel. What we feel, though important, is relative,
not subject to norms or laws. What we know is what is
capable of being measured. Only what is measurable
is true, capable of being known. There is one truth --
that which is measurable -- but there are many values
and cultures. Culture is a set of meanings and values
informing a way of life. Each culture should be valued
for what it is. No one culture and value is better
than another. Humans can understand many things, but

21

we must realize that their understanding develops
over time. Truth is one but we continually know that
truth. It is only in knowing that truth, little by
little, that we advance and gain more knowledge about
the world and its realities. Our source of truth is
the world around us as seen through modern methods of
investigation. To say otherwise is to refuse to recognize the obvious. All truth is temporal and historical in character. It is in process and relative to
other events and people. Education is not being told
the truth; rather, it is discovering, through dialogue, the truth we share. Education presents methods
for use in the continual investigation of what is true
and how to act. If we learn how to investigate, we
will be on the road to a continual process of learning.
If we follow the modern way our life will have variety,
joy, change, and, as a consequence, a never-ending
taste for the new, the good, the vitally alive.

This description of change from the classical
worldview to the modern worldview is a common one.
If the description is accurate it is also a description of radical change. All that remains in common
between the two eras are the constitutive elements.
The challenge for those who live in the post-modern
era is to understand the other eras or pasts. To
fail to understand is to fail to know what true
options were taken in the past. We live in the light
of those past choices.

Change and the Church

The 16th century saw the beginning of the challenge of the modern way of life. But the challenge
itself peaked in the late 19th and early 20th centuries.

Significant changes occurred outside the Catholic
Church during the 19th and 20th centuries. Democracy,
Republicanism, and Socialism became the political
system of most countries in the world. The challenge
of Enlightenment thought intensified with the work of
individuals like Darwin, Marx and Freud. Evolution
as a biological theory and then as a systematic
approach to life challenged the understanding of human
nature, the world, and even God as static, finished

and known. Evolution suggested that change is inherent
to the understanding and essence of everything. The
socioeconomic theory developed by Marx described the
place of religion in the social structure. Perhaps,
he suggested, the Church is actually defending the
status quo. Her doctrine, sacraments and present
organizational structure are ways to keep one class
in power. Perhaps religion is used by those in power
to subjugate the poor. Freud looked not at social
structure but at psychic structure: Our thoughts,
feelings, and reactions all are determined by the
inner working of our subconscious and its various
parts. Religion is the way people cope with life.
Instead of looking at life the way it is, people
created religion to look at it the way it should be.
Religion and God are all illusion, said Freud. Historians began to investigate the Bible the way they
investigated any other piece of literature. In the
process, they discovered that it was not written when
churchmen claimed it was. Rather, it was a book containing various types of literature and thus was not
all history, and finally, that history as written by
the authors of the Bible was not like history which
he modern historian writes. The Bible was challenged.

These challenges of mind and government were evident in the Western world. Some groups of Protestants
examined them, found some truth in them, and consequent-
y accepted them into their religious life. Other
Protestants rejected them completely. These latter,
the Fundamentalist Christians, introduced a new view of
he Bible. They claimed it alone was literally God's
ords and anything that challenged it should be reject-
d. It was infallible. They would have nothing to do
ith the new history, psychology, biology, and social
heories.

The Catholic Church, much like the Fundamentalist
Protestants, found it difficult to deal with the developments of the 19th and 20th centuries. It grudgingly
accepted the political change but did not see the
pluralistic modern state as a goal for humanity. Instead, it held that the ideal society would be when
religion, political life and cultural life were one.
he ideal was still the Golden Age of Medieval

Christianity. Intellectually this was also the thought process most favored in the Catholic Church. The thought of the medieval theologian St. Thomas Aquinas was showered with favors. It became the basis for turn-of-the-century Catholicism facing the challenges outside its way of life. Anyone who accepted the prevalent thought of the Western world as a model for theologizing was denied the title of Catholic Theologian.

An example of this rejection is found in the condemnation of "Americanism." Pope Leo XIII's letter of condemnation in 1899 warned against the values of self-initiative, democracy, and freedom as a part of Church life. A movement entitled "Modernism" was also condemned in 1907 by Pius X. All Catholic priests were compelled to take an oath against it. This condemnation and oath rejected evolution and the rise of historical criteria in biblical studies and demanded acceptance of miracles, of an unchanging truth throughout time, and an inerrant papacy. These condemnations and the fervent rooting out of anyone who might adhere to "modern" thought processes resulted in a peculiar American Catholic view of contemporary life that favored the pre-modern or classical past as the model for the future.

When the Church disintegrated as the soul of European culture it was faced with the beginning of the modern world. After the disintegration of the Medieval Church Roman Catholicism looked back with a deep yearning for the times of Establishment. The Council of Trent (1545-63) reformed the Church in the classic medieval form, lessening the tension between the ideals and the facts, but the ideals were still from the Middle Ages. Even though Trent minimized the tension between the ideals and the facts, the Church was still faced with the challenges posed by modernity, including a questioning of the authenticity of the ideals themselves. The modern way of life challenged Catholicism as identified with the Medieval Church. The Church authorities, until recently, had been against those basic changes in thought and organization described as modern. However, since Vatican II (1962-65), modernity has once again become a viable choice for Catholic living.

THE PAST AS IMMIGRATION 1830-1930

An immigrant comes with bags packed from his past, ready to work in the present with hope for a future life. An immigrant leaves his or her native land for a new life, a life different from that found at home. He or she builds dreams of the future with vague hopes and scant information. But the immigrant still leaves one way of life to find a better one.

Any Church with an international mission is an immigrant. It is never comfortable with the way life is. Life can always be better. The Church has no homeland since its goal is to be "at home" in every culture. But to be at home it must undergo a time of immigrancy status. Each period of immigrancy is different as the Church, present where Christians gather together, enters into the life of a new nation. The story of the immigrant Roman Catholic Church reflects the uniqueness of the United States, which, until recently, was considered a Protestant country.

It was Protestant even though Spanish Catholics discovered and first settled the Caribbean and reached the extreme Southeast and Southwest of what was to become the United States. French Catholics clearly dominated the Northeast during the first centuries of discovery. In the end, however, they were centered in Canada and not in the United States. In 1776 there were only 30,000 Catholics in a U.S. population of several million. These Catholics were accepted as supporters of the revolution yet were suspected of having false motives. They, like the Jews, blacks, and native Americans, were hyphenated Americans. They were French-Americans, Irish-Americans, Italian-Americans. This hyphen indicated that they lived as guests of their hosts, the Americans. The struggle of this past of American Roman Catholics is the struggle of many Catholic peoples to share the past of the United States and offer Protestant America an opportunity to share a Catholic past. This mutual sharing is only presently being accomplished.

Between 1830 and 1930 the Church in America made a new beginning. This country's gradual westward expansion met the already established but weak Hispanic Catholicism of the Southwestern United States and California. The successive waves of immigrants from Europe hit American shores with new languages, cultures, and values. From a small, aristocratic, rural, educated Catholicism of revolutionary times the Church became a large, poor, urban, uneducated mass of people. Ireland and Germany alone sent over two million immigrants in the 1850's.

Westward expansion and immigrant numbers presented four challenges to the immigrant Church: 1) What should be done with so many people? 2) How should the Church cope with the diverse cultures? 3) Should it accept and adopt the American way of life in its organizational forms and theological expressions? 4) How should the Church respond to the Anglo-American's rejection of the European immigrant and the western Hispanic Catholic? The Church's response to these challenges determined how long and how intense she would be considered and consider herself immigrant.

How the Church dealt with increased population

The Church responded to the challenge of growth through building schools, orphanages, hospitals, and social service agencies, supporting   labor movements, and doing whatever else it could to protect the immigrant from a hostile environment.

The Catholic school system came into existence because the public schools of the mid-19th century were Protestant. It was not unusual before the Civil War to have a Protestant catechism used as a reading text, Protestant hymns sung in class, or the King James version of the Bible read in the public schools. The history books of the time referred to Protestants as Americans and Catholics as "them." The Catholic Church was portrayed as an oppressive, superstitious, anti-Christian institution. Beginning with the first Catholic school founded by the Ursuline Sisters in New Orleans in 1727, religious orders formed their

26

own schools to give Catholic children an education and a sense of religious worth. Without their dedication and learning, the Church as we know it would not exist. While leading a life of prayer and physical sacrifice, these orders taught their fellow Catholics and educated themselves. The schools, like everything else in American Catholicism, were a source of division as well as unity from the very beginning. They posed questions such as should we change the public school system or start our own? Should we spend money on Catholic school children or on Catholics in the public schools? Should the schools reflect the views and values of the local Catholic community or of the bishop? This last question is a reflection of the struggle between the American hierarchy and national parishes. No matter what the tension or how prolonged the battle, schools became essential to immigrant American Catholicism.

Catholics also founded orphanages, hospitals, and social service agencies for use by fellow Catholics. Orphanages were necessary because of the destruction of Catholic families through sickness, death, movement of men out of the cities to find work, or separation during the voyage from Europe. Catholic hospitals respected the language, traditions, and religious values of their people while providing a place where the customs of the seriously ill were recognized. Parishes acted as centers of employment as well as support for the unemployed.

Catholics, for the most part, provided the cheap labor to run the mills and factories. Used, abused, and discarded when no longer necessary, these laborers were often viewed as having less value than machines. Labor attempted to organize during the 19th century but failed because unions were perceived as threats to the American way of life. However, the Catholic Church in the United States became identified with the labor movement because a few influential bishops supported the attempt of the large number of Catholic laborers for unions.

Catholic Homelands, Catholic Church

Catholics protected themselves by living together. Parish life became the focus of Catholicism. The parish offered familiar language, customs, saints, and worship. Whether it was the silent Mass of the Irish parishes, the ornate sung Mass of the Germans, or the extroverted processions of the Sicilians, the worship familiar to the immigrants could be found in their parishes.

One may have belonged to a "national parish," or a "geographical parish." The geographical parish was marked by physical boundaries such as streets, or county or state lines. All Catholics within those geographical lines were members of the parish. The national parish was constituted by all those belonging to the same ethnic group. Residence in a certain geographical area was not required. The conflict between these two types of parishes was long and arduous: those supporting the National claimed that Catholicism could not survive unless those of like background, language, and expectations belonged to the same parish. The geographical-parish concept was favored to instill unity of the Church under one bishop. This latter concept of parish caused an international crisis in 1890 when Peter Paul Cahensely, a German layman, claimed that the Irish-American bishops were attempting to destroy the faith of German immigrants by forcing them into English-speaking parish life. This issue was never legally resolved. Instead, more bishops with specific ethnic backgrounds and linguistic abilities were appointed to dioceses throughout the United States.

The solution to the parish problem was one example of the continuing difficulty of matching people's desires and episcopal competence. Each new wave of immigration posed new challenges. The first wave of immigrants thought its way of life was Catholicism. Each identified itself as the Church. The educated and rich English Catholics, who were first, had a difficult time understanding the Irish-Catholic; the Irish, in understanding the French; the French, the German; the German, the Italian. Examples abound.

Irish parishioners complained about French priests who hardly spoke their language and gave pedantic and esoteric sermons. The French parishioners, on the other hand, complained about the language and moralistic sermons of the Irish. We find Irish bishops looking at the Sicilian customs of processions and feasts as superstitious and more reminiscent of paganism than of Catholicism. All of these immigrants looked at the Catholicism of the Southwest as a sporadic, unenthusiastic remnant of centuries-old missionary activity. The Irish were the largest immigrant Catholic group in turn-of-the-century America, and many Irish men and women became priests and nuns. As a consequence, the Irish rose to power and were responsible for the Church's adaptation to American life and movement away from being an immigrant church.

American Church; American Way of Life?

The Protestant American society in which the immigrant Catholic Church existed did not reflect the Protestantism of Luther or Calvin as much as that of the Puritans, Quakers, and other radical reformers. This style of Protestantism favored the individualism of conscience over the communalism of society, interior piety over exterior liturgy, Bible over custom and history. These aspects of radical Protestantism were reflected in America's Constitution and Bill of Rights. European Catholicism had a difficult time understanding both the Protestantism and the Bill of Rights of the United States, while American Catholicism was divided over such issues as democratic freedom and openness to the Protestant Churches.

The first significant argument over adapting to democratic freedom was "lay trusteeism." A common practice among Protestants was to incorporate church property in the name of the laity. Some states would not permit a church as such to own property. Obviously, this was a question of developing American law, American democracy, and the Church's ability to adapt to both. Bishop John Carroll (1735-1815), the first American bishop, allowed the practice of lay trustees, but refused to permit lay people to hire or dismiss their priests. Such practices were easy to legislate but difficult to enforce. During this time priests were so scarce that it was not unusual for lay people to band together and search for a priest either in the United States or in Europe. Once the priest came, the people felt they should have a say in accepting or rejecting him. The practice of lay trusteeism caused so much anxiety and friction that it was condemned by American bishops in the first Provincial Council of Baltimore in 1829. With this condemnation the involvement and control of the laity in the affairs of the Church died. The bishops ruled everything. Only Bishop John England (1820-1842) of Charleston, South Carolina, attempted to have assemblies of laity and clergy advising him on church affairs. Not until after Vatican II has any bishop followed in his footsteps.

The Church made other attempts at becoming American toward the end of the 19th century. Many small groups of Catholics made pleas for the elimination of clerical celibacy, clerical dress, the Latin Mass, and the value of accepting the freedoms in the Bill of Rights. These attempts to Americanize the Church, though loud, failed, with failure institutionalized by the Third Plenary Council of Baltimore in 1884. The term Ghetto Catholicism refers to the Church in the spirit of this Council. Ghetto Catholicism was marked by its defensiveness, clericalism, separation from other Americans, deepening of Tridentine customs, and devotion to the papacy. Ghetto Catholicism and American immigrant Catholicism are synonymous.

Immigrant Catholicism's defensiveness was manifest in the growth of publications which stated the Catholic position about topics ranging from women's dress to making war. The manner in which the priest accepted responsibility for every detail of church life demonstrates <u>clericalism</u>. The priest was the center of Catholic life. His ability to forgive sins in confession, bring Jesus down to the altar at the Mass, and solve the problems of the immigrant community placed him in a position of power and honor.

To set Catholics apart from other Americans,

immigrant Catholicism forbade them from praying with Protestants. Such a command was easy to obey since Catholics lived in the same neighborhoods and had few chances to associate with Protestants. Marriage to a Protestant and attendance at a Protestant service were viewed as sinful. It was even wrong for a priest to offer a prayer from the same podium as a Protestant minister at a religious, political or sports event.

The immigrants came to the United States wedded to many devotions and practices which pre-dated Trent (1545-63). As the clergy became more educated through the seminary system, they were molded in the tradition of the Council of Trent. The years after Trent were the first time the papacy had such total control over the priests. The commission in charge of seminaries established the curricula, formation programs, and spiritual exercises in the Tridentine, and later the Vatican I tradition. Seminary education placed emphasis on saying the rosary, devotion to the Saints, Mary, the Sacred Heart, Novenas, Masses without a congregation (private Masses), and the presence of Jesus in the Eucharistic bread. The result was the mixture of immigrant devotions with the devotions preached by the clergy.

The kind of devotion to the papacy which developed during the 19th and 20th centuries is central to understanding the American Church. At various times the Pope had been seen as a simple apostle, the bishop of the diocese of Rome, the Patriarch of the West, the Lord of the Papal States, the head of Christendom. After the French Revolution, however, a devotion developed among the common people which focused upon the Pope as a symbol of their Catholicism, the director of their Catholic life and the visible presence of God among them. This devotional and populist papacy began with Pius VII's (1800-1823) struggle with Napoleon and was finalized in its present form by Pius IX (1846-1878) in the decrees on infallibility. This decree, as popularized by the press, made infallibility the same as divine inspiration. It became the mark of good Catholics to think as the Pope thought and to act as the Pope wished them to act. The Pope became the Church; the Church, the Pope.

Devotion to the papacy fit the needs of the immigrant Catholic. It reached beyond the hatred of the Protestants, beyond the squalid conditions of their life and beyond the diverse customs and values to one who stood above the storm. This person, dressed in white, was God's presence among them, giving answers and direction to Catholic life in all parts of the world. The papacy itself was shaped by the needs of the time. It, in turn, shaped the times and the Church.

These were the internal challenges and forms of immigrant Catholicism. The large influx of immigrants, coping with their own values and culture, challenged Americanism in all its forms. The Church which developed as a consequence was independent of the surrounding culture and her people were convinced that life within her rule and realm was the good life. Meanwhile, many non-Catholics challenged the Church's authenticity as a Christian Church and its viability as an American institution. These people saw themselves as the true Americans.

Americanism

Catholics threatened the Protestant American way of life socially, politically, economically and religiously. Religiously, Catholics belonged to a Church the early Puritans hated, the revivalists shook their fist at, and Protestants protested against. Economically, the Catholics provided cheap labor or were jobless and dependent on charity. Politically, they challenged the old politics of the social and intellectual elite. Americans feared that the democratic institutions of America would be overrun by these people who had never known democracy and whose Church in Europe preached against it. Socially, the urban concentration of immigrants threatened the traditional agrarian patterns of American life. To the Protestants, the cities were sources of wickedness, drunkenness, and Catholics.

This perceived threat was not taken lightly. Protestant anti-Catholics sought to protect their society through propaganda which said that nuns were

prostitutes for priests and that the Pope was planning
to use the Catholics to take over the country. As a
result, mobs burned convents and roamed city streets
burning churches and killing Catholics. This fear of
Catholicism resulted in a movement known as
Nativism and a political party known as the American
or Know-Nothing Party. The Nativists claimed to be
true Americans, the Americans immigrants should imitate if they wished to live in this country. The
Know-Nothings were a coalition of pro-slavery groups,
secret societies, working men's organizations, and
militant Protestants who hated Catholics. In 1855
five states had Know-Nothing Legislatures; five others
had Legislatures with a near majority. 75 Know-
Nothings were elected to Congress. The Civil War
brought an end to the Know-Nothing Party but not an
end to the inherent distrust of Catholics in the United
States. This inherent distrust of Catholics has led
historians such as Arthur Schlesinger, Sr. to say,
"I regard prejudice against the Church as the deepest
bias in the history of the American people." Some
still wonder if this bias is present among non-Catholics who reject any form of Catholic values and agenda
for political action.

     In response to this prejudice, Catholics tried to
prove themselves true Americans. Catholic blood was
spilt and Catholic men demonstrated bravery in all the
wars of the United States. Catholics were evident in
many of the national sports: Gene Tunney in boxing;
Babe Ruth in baseball; Knute Rockne in football.
Notre Dame was the symbol of Catholic America: blue-
collar Catholics defeating through brawn and brain
Ivy League Protestants. But Catholics were not American enough to be accepted by the national voters.
When Alfred E. Smith ran for president in 1928, he
lost to Herbert Hoover, with Smith's Catholicism a
major topic in the campaign.

     Catholicism reflected American institutions in
miniature. There were Catholic Boy Scouts, bowling
leagues, lawyer guilds, and even Catholic approved
films.

     The immigrant way of life resulted in a feeling

of unity, a sense of purpose, and a common identity.
Catholics did not eat meat on Friday. They blessed
themselves when walking in front of their churches,
wore uniforms to school, and treated their sisters
and priests with respect. One of the greatest honors
in a Catholic family was to have a son become a priest
or brother or a daughter a nun. Protestants might not
like Catholics. Catholics, however, were secure in
their belief that what their priest taught them was
true and that the family who prayed together stayed
together.

Catholicism before World War II was disciplined,
strong, self-sacrificing, dedicated and united. Much
of this self-sacrifice, dedication and sense of purpose
was found in its missionary outreach both at home and
in foreign lands. At the beginning of the 20th century
Protestants seldom converted to Catholicism. After
1930, however, the number of conversions increased.
Some converted because the Church demanded that the
children of an interdenominational marriage be raised
Catholic; others, because Catholics began to talk and
preach their faith in non-Catholic areas. The preaching was so intense that a joke was going around in the
1920's that Catholics called each other "Mac" because
it stood for "Make America Catholic." American Catholics also supported a great deal of missionary activity
outside the U.S.A. The Maryknoll, for instance, was
founded for the specific purpose of American missionary
work in foreign lands. A system of funding developed
which reached into every Catholic school through such
techniques as "buying babies," in which Catholic
children gathered monies to support the care and wel-
fare of those children the missionaries were serving.

As Catholics sent their sons to war they were
secure in their faith, confident of their abilities,
fearful of their economic security. Those who returned alive from the war and those who remained
at home became the foundation of another dimension
of the Catholic Church in the United States. From a
Church which was urban, poor, uneducated, and immigrant, the American Church became one which was
suburban, middle class, educated, and increasingly

recognized as American. This latter Church is closer to the present Church than to that of the past.

THE PAST IN THE PRESENT: A CONCLUSION FOR NOW

The present is the past transformed by life. The Church of beginnings, establishment, change, and immigrants is dead. This moment, now, is spent by the living who remember the dead. We are the Church of the living and the dead; the past, the present, and the future. The past is found among us in fact and challenge.

The Church's beginnings are transformed by present life: the Jewish synagogue service and meal of friendship which became our Mass is still with us in American folk song; priestly preaching, churches with pews, and American bread and wine. We address God as Father, aware of the psychological dimensions of fatherhood and the linguistic challenge of the women's movement. We retain an organizational structure that is sensitive to the tension between democratic desires and bureaucratic restriction. These are the facts. The beginnings of Jerusalem, Greece, and Rome are still with us, but they participate in the challenge of beginning again in a new land and at a critically different time.

The Church of the Middle Ages is fresh in our collective memory. It became the Tridentine Church, a Church that opposed Protestantism and yearned for the Middle Ages. Protestantism looked to the Golden Age of the Bible for its model of Christianity; Catholicism looked to the Feudalism of the Middle Ages. The Council of Trent (1545-1563) took the challenges of the Protestants, if not the times, as an impetus for a reform. The bishops gathered at Trent to respond to what they understood as the Protestant vision and the Catholic abuses. In rejecting both vision and abuses, the Council of Trent shaped the Catholic view of reform and adaptation until the second Vatican Council (1962-65).

The response was disciplinary and dogmatic. Trent established seminaries for the training of priests, forbade bishops to rule more than one diocese, and certified as valid only those marriages witnessed by one's pastor or delegate. These and many other decrees provided the legal machinery for ridding the Church of abuse. The Council also placed the responsibility for reform in papal hands, increasing the centralization of the Church. Many of the central bureaus still in existence for governing the Church were established in 1588 by Sixtus V. The dogmatic response as formulated in the centuries after the Council was argumentative and anti-Protestant. Although there was diversity of opinion at the Council and the Council did not want to restrict the theological discussion of those days, the Church became more narrow in theological options subsequent to the Council.

The Catholic stance favored priest and Pope over minister and Bible. The rituals of the sacraments were stripped of abuses and made uniform in administration. Against the Protestant emphasis on simplicity and the language of the people, the Catholics fostered Latin and complex ritual. Where the Protestant looked to the Bible for direction in life, the Catholic looked to both the Bible and the historical tradition of Christianity. Finally, the Protestant emphasis upon faith was countered by a Catholic renewal of devotional works emphasizing novenas, rosary, saints, Mary, and the presence of Jesus in the Eucharist. Trent was a turning point for Roman Catholicism. It turned the Church's back on the Protestants and committed Catholics to increased centralization, strong defensive theologies, and a continuation of the Medieval tradition.

Both the Tridentine Church and the Immigrant Church passed away after the Second World War. These ways of life died not because of ill will nor antipathy, but because people change. Immigrant sons and daughters went to college in large numbers. The G.I. Bill paid for some; blue collar salaries resulting from increased unionization paid for others. College exposed them to the ideas of the Enlightenment, the social sciences, and the new philosophies. It moved them into the mainstream of American living. Increased economic status found them in the suburbs, many times next door to Protestants. The suburban parish reflected new interests: family, comfort, pragmatic religion, and a desire to increase their standard of living. The parish was one of the many organizations they belonged to; their religion, one of the many ways of life they were exposed to; their liturgy, one isolated moment in a week concerned with those values inherent to the American way of life.

New ways of life, new ideas, and new people caused the Church to have new problems. As the flood of immigrants challenged the Church in the 19th and early 20th centuries, so the movement of educated, highly mobile, middle class people to the suburbs challenged her after World War II.

The reality of Trent and the immigrant Church are still with us. Significant segments of the American Catholic Church look to these pasts as sources of literal imitation for the present. If we do not live, speak and act as the Catholic of these pasts, some Catholics feel we reject our past and, consequently, our Catholicism. The challenge for everyone is how to remember these pasts in a Church which is undergoing significant change.

We have changed as a Church. People in the United States share the mentality which saw the passing of both the classical and modern age. Since 1960 the Catholic Church has been caught in a vortex of pasts swirling around, catching us in their force and attractiveness. In the short space of 20 years Catholics faced the ecclesiastical challenges that had accumulated over the previous two hundred. Once we agreed there was value to modern, democratic, middle-class life, we then had to face the necessity of discovering that value. The major Protestant faiths went through the turmoil of change throughout the 19th and 20th centuries. We began in the sixties and continue today. Our challenge in the face of these changes is not to repeat the mistakes of those who have gone before us but to begin again in the new age with the spirit of the first Christians and the experience of 2000 years.

The immigrant past is with us today among Hispanics and Asian Catholics. One part of our Catholic
Church is identified with American life while another
segment is not. The immigrant diversity expressed
so well in the diversity of parishes is the challenge
of today. Without ethnic solidarity how do we become
a Catholic community in the sprawling suburbs? How
do we become a Catholic community while we are part
immigrant Church and part American Church with an
immigrant past?

These are some of our pasts which enliven the
present. The present finds us the largest single
denomination in the United States -- approximately
50 million strong. We are found in every state in
the Union, but especially in the Southwest, southern
Texas, the Delta country of Louisiana, and New England. The cities of the Northeast and Great Lakes
find Catholics dominating their politics and culture.

The present Church is characterized by diversity.
The number and geography just mentioned reflect a
pluralistic Church, a Church of options, a Church
characterized by diversity in ethnicity, in theologies, and in visions for the future.

The ethnic diversity is reflected in two significant communities: the European, which includes the
Irish, and the Hispanic, which includes all those
dependent upon Hispanic culture both present and past.

There are significant differences between these
Roman Catholic communities and within each of them.
What we mention here is only a hint at the plurality
of ideas, values, customs, and ways of living in
today's Church.

The overwhelming majority of the 50 million
Roman Catholics in the United States came here as
immigrants in the 19th and 20th centuries. Many
Catholics will have their roots in these immigrant
communities. While retaining such roots, they have
risen educationally and economically more swiftly
than any other immigrant group except the Jews.

All the evidence indicates that whereas the media portray Catholic ethnics as blue collar, hardhat, racist, prejudiced, uneducated, conservative, and self-centered, the facts, as demonstrated in Greeley's American Catholic, show them as white collar, less prejudiced than their Protestant counterparts, and liberal on bread and butter issues and service to the poor.

The same mismatch can be seen among the Hispanics. They comprise about 25 percent of the Church in the United States. About 58 percent are blue collar workers, while only 5 percent are farm laborers; 85 percent of Hispanic Catholics live in the cities, while 21 percent are well below the poverty level. The demand of Hispanic Catholics at present is for jobs and advancement equivalent to their education. While 57 percent of those between the ages of 25 and 29 have completed high school, they have not advanced economically according to their education and experience. Although Hispanic Catholics make up a large portion of the Church, they are not well represented among the clergy and religious. The reasons for this seem to reside in the prejudice of the non-Hispanic majority toward the Hispanic way of living Catholicism. Certainly the future of the Church in the United States will be lived with a much stronger Hispanic influence.

Such diversity exists in the United States, yet it is not necessarily recognized either by Church members themselves or the interpreters of American life, the media. One stereotype for both Church officials and media is that the Church is a group of people who are middle-class, suburban Americans. This is true of only one portion of American Catholics. We must be sensitive to this partial truth because the media determine how we see ourselves and our past. American Roman Catholicism reflects all the Catholic cultures of the world.

Diversity in Theologies

A Catholic theology attempts to understand and describe the Catholic version of life. Catholicism

in the United States has a plurality of theologies
just as it has a variety of pasts and cultures. Each
theology attempts to articulate a clear description
and understanding of Catholic faith and doctrine.
Every gathering of Catholics finds these theologies
in use.

For instance, many dioceses in the United States
encourage parishes to form parish councils, groups of
parishioners who assist the clergy and the parish
community in making decisions about those goals and
daily activities which form the parish. The view-
points of these new theologies can be found represented
at any parish council meeting: a discussion about
parish finances finds some members urging that the
money be spent on the parish buildings, while others
want to spend it serving the poor, preaching the gospel
message, or promoting the interior life and spirituality of the parishioners. Each of these positions,
argued so well and clearly, are actually different
ways of understanding what the role of the Church is
in our world: to provide a permanent place (building)
to serve people's "religious" needs; to free those
bound by society's injustice; to evangelize the
secular world; to bring us close to each other and
our God in a loving community. These people, gathered
together in a local parish council, represent some
of the theologies in the American Church. Many others
are described in this book.

Diversity of Dreams for the Future

The different visions of life are hopes of what
Catholicism should be. Each suggests what is wrong
with our present world, describes how the past helps
us understand our present situation, and looks toward
a time when Catholicism, as described and understood
by the particular ideal, will authenticate itself.

Such plurality of visions along with the lack of
an overarching vision leaves Roman Catholicism in an
identity crisis. A strong conflict exists between
those who wish the plurality of visions to remain
in the Church and those who are convinced that without
a uniformity of vision, the Church will disintegrate.

Such a tension over Catholic identity presupposes a number of issues, all vitally important and worth reflecting on regarding the present concerns of the Church. Authentic tension presupposes an awareness of a past which gave joy and meaning to all who have gone before us; a sensitivity to the present in knowing what is occurring in the Church today; and a willingness to continue with the Church into an unknown future. It also presupposes concern, not one shown by anger or boredom, two ways to react to crisis situations, but by knowing the options and intelligently choosing and living one of them. The future will have its history, a history that we choose now. Our return to the past creates history in the present. We search for a usable past so that we will have a usable future. We search in the past for those memories which help us understand the "why" of how we should live.

QUESTIONS

Questions of three types follow each chapter: those for personal reflection, which give each student suggestions for thought, those for group reflection and discussion; and review questions. Those for personal reflection are not to be shared in a group, but should be thought about and answered, in diary form, in private.

Personal Reflection

1. If you were Joseph or Ann, what would you wish from your Church?

2. The early Christians had many options, but basically they could join or leave the Church. Would you ever leave the Church? What keeps you in the Church? What could possibly provide you with what the Church provides? Does it challenge you?

3. Is your view of Roman Catholicism Established or open to change?

4. Ask three people of different ages what they like or dislike about the Church's worship, organization, and belief.

5. Which of the pasts do you think is the best reflection of Catholicism? What is the basis of your decision?

Group Discussion

1. What do Catholics today have in common with the Church of beginnings? How do they differ?

2. Is it good for a nation to have one Church as Europe did during the Middle Ages?

3. Share the results of your questioning the three people, as requested in 4. above.

4. If you had to choose between the classical and modern view, which would you choose? Do you think both could be improved on? How?

5. If you had to live during one of the Church's pasts, which would you choose and why?

Review Questions

1. Look up Vatican Council II in the Catholic Encyclopedia or another reference book and answer the following questions: When was it? Who was pope? What was the most significant effect it had upon Roman Catholic worship, church organization, belief, and relationship with non-Catholics?

2. Name three beginnings of the Church and show the influence of these beginnings upon worship, organization, and belief.

3. Describe the Medieval world view.

4. Compare the pre-modern and modern ways of life. How do they influence contemporary Catholicism?

5. How did the Immigrant Church care for the Catholic
    immigrant?

6. How diverse is present-day Catholicism?

SUGGESTED READINGS

Abbott, Walter; Gallagher,
Joseph
The Documents of Vatican II
America Press 1966

An excellent compi-
lation of Vatican
II Documents with
commentary by par-
ticipants.

Aubert, Robert, ed.
Christian Centuries: The
Church in a Secularized Society
Paulist 1978

The Christian Cen-
tury Series is one
of the better aca-
demic Church histor-
ies in English.

Bokenkotter, Thomas A.
Concise History of the Catholic
Church
Doubleday 1977

An excellent one-
volume history of
the Church.

Brophy, Don and Westenhaver,
Edythe, eds.
The Story of Catholics in America
Paulist 1978

A short, popular
account of American
Catholicism.

Danielou, Jean; Marrou, Henri
Christian Centuries: First Six
Hundred Years
Paulist, 1969

The Church of
Beginnings

Foy, Felician
The Catholic Almanac
Our Sunday Vicitor Inc.

The Almanac is a
short compilation of
"Catholic" facts and
figures for the
previous year.

Greeley, Andrew
The American Catholic: A
Social Portrait
Basic Books 1977

A much-needed socio-
logical analysis of
those who call them-
selves Roman Catholic
in the United States.

Hennesey, James
American Catholics
Oxford University Press, 1981

The best history of
American Catholicism
published today.

II. WORD(S) OF GOD: REVELATION

LEN BIALLAS

Recently some friends were married in a neighbor's back yard. The couple wanted an outdoor ceremony rather than one in a traditional setting with an organ, white carpet, and fancy ushers. They felt such traditional trappings did not mean anything. They detracted from the presence of God which, they believed, pervaded a simple garden ceremony amid flowers and other beauties of nature.

I would never have noticed this wedding if it did not contrast with another recent experience. While enjoying breakfast in a restaurant my wife and I overheard a conversation between a truck driver and two rabbit hunters. The truck driver had just read a popular book describing the end of the world. He was convinced that the end was coming, and that predictions of the scriptures would be fulfilled. Christians would be "caught up in the clouds to meet the Lord in the air." The truck driver was trying to persuade the two hunters that Russia was the incarnation of the devil. Russia, he said, was the beast that the book of Revelation warns Christians is the sign of impending Judgment.

What makes these two episodes so interesting is that they represent two extremes of a common, if mistaken, Christian belief about the presence of God. For the married couple, nothing could detract from their feeling that God is everywhere -- in gardens, in sunsets, in all of nature. For the truck driver, God is present only in the Second Coming of Christ. It was as if he could draw a portrait of what Christ would look like. The final battle of the New Testament was more than vivid pictorial language for him -- it was cold, hard reality, and about to happen.

In contrast, Roman Catholic doctrine asserts that God became a human being and dwelt among us. In so

doing, God subjected the revelation of Himself to
the limitations and rich possibilities of human symbolism. God revealed himself fully in a human being,
Jesus in the Incarnation. From then on, Catholics
believe, God is present in a diversity of ways.
In a real sense both the newlyweds and the truck driver
refuse to take the Incarnation of God in Jesus with
full seriousness. To insist that God is present in
nature (and thus everywhere) or only at the Second
Coming (and thus only in some vivid, magical, crowd-
pleasing fashion) is to limit the activity of the
Christian God.

Revelation As Presence

Over the centuries Roman Catholics stressed one
of the forms of revelation of God to the exclusion
of other forms of presence. By their emphasis on the
real presence of Jesus in the Eucharist, they are not
far from the truck driver in narrowing the ways in
which God reveals Himself to us. While granting lip-
service to Vatican II's teaching that the presence of
Christ is primarily to the Church, and thus in the
believer, the worshipper, the community, the priest,
and the word of the Gospel, Catholics still emphasize
one form of real presence -- in the Eucharist.

To be sure, the scriptures affirm the sacramental
presence of Christ as it is celebrated daily in the
Church (cf. chapter 6 of John's Gospel or chapter 11
of Paul's first letter to the Corinthians). Catholics
rightly share the conviction that the liturgical
celebration of Christ's life evokes and makes present
the power and effect of the historical events of His
life. This presence is effective to the extent that
it is directed toward the union between Christ and
believers. Yet this real presence creates a paradox,
for the revelation of God in the real presence of
Christ comes about not through a physical presence,
but precisely through a physical absence. In the
Eucharist, there is a personal presence of Jesus, but
this is a type of presence which is humanly much more
"real" than mere physical presence.

In human encounters the essence of personal presence does not require that persons be close to each other spatially. Even in separation persons can be close to each other. I can talk to my wife on the phone, be in the same room with her, think about her, talk about her -- all these are forms of real presence. Indeed, even physical absence can be a form of presence. Physical presence does not necessarily mean real presence. When one person is ignored or rejected, for example, there is not a full personal presence of one to another. The essense of personal presence demands a free communication of the self and a spiritual openness to the other person, and it allows a rich variety of modes of expression.

Thinking of Christ as present only in the Eucharist ignores the rich variety of degrees of real presence. In fact, Christ's presence in the Christian community goes beyond a bodily, earthly, or spatial relationship to this world. His presence in the community, His glorified bodily reality because of the resurrection, is of a totally different order than mere physical presence. Christ is present where His activity is present. This takes many forms.

In its Constitution on the Sacred Liturgy, Vatican II stressed thet Christ is always present in the Church. The Fathers situated the real presence of Christ in the Eucharist within a much broader context. They placed it in the context cf a wider appreciation of His real presence to the Church in all the actions in which it continues Christ's saving work: "By His power, He is present in the sacraments, so that when someone baptizes, it is Christ Himself who baptizes. He is present in His word, since it is He Himself who speaks when the holy scriptures are read in the Church. He is present, finally, when the Church prays and sings, for he promised: 'where two or three are gathered together for My sake, there I am in the midst of them.' (<u>Sac. Lit., art. 7</u>)

In this chapter we will concentrate on one form of real presence mentioned by Vatican II. We will focus on His presence in scripture, the word of God, where Jesus manifests Himself fully. A glance at the revelation of God in scripture will show us still other forms of His real presence.

The Bible as Revelation

Protestants stress that the Bible is the "word of God." They have always given the Bible a place of prominence in their rituals, the place par excellence where God is to be heard and responded to. In the last 40 years Catholics, with Vatican II as one of the principal stimuli, are rediscovering this presence of God in the Bible. Today they are recognizing more and more that Jesus, the "Word of God," mediates the love and power of God not only through the Eucharist but also through the scriptures.

People today are often wary of words and prefer a new language of the non-word: touch, dance, music. Slips of the tongue, they say, often tell us more than ordinary speech, and silence can speak louder than words. Sometimes words are to be understood literally, sometimes symbolically, and sometimes both. Still, the Bible is the "Word of God," a symbolic manifestation of God's personal relationship with His people. It is a record of His actions of love to the early Christian community, the proclamation of the Good News of His mercy.

If we can get a better understanding of what the basic message of the Bible is, then it will prove to be a boon rather than an obstacle to mature faith. It will take a prominent place in individual lives. But how are we to approach the Bible to see the essential part it plays in the Catholic heritage? Biblical scholars may be of some help. Though their language is sometimes technical and highly specialized, their vast scholarship and investigations cannot simply be ignored. They can help us meditate on the deep riches of scripture. Scholars show us that the Bible is anything but a treasure chest of proof texts: a book where the answers are known before it is consulted. These scholars keep us from blindly accepting every word as literal, an approach which often leads to contradictions and mental anguish. They insist that a proper interpretation of the Bible always entails and involves living out a commitment to the God who invites us to share that divine life which is the essence of His heritage.

Without becoming involved in the debates of scholars, we do want to utilize the fruits of their investigations to further our own understanding of the Bible. If nothing else, they prod us to recognize that passages of scripture, taken out of context, can be made to express anything we want -- and perhaps very different messages from the original Biblical authors and editors. Proper interpretation of the Bible entails reflection on the significant issues of community experiences, which every Catholic is called to participate in. This does not mean that the Bible has the answers to all our questions. It does mean that the Bible gives the basic symbols which Catholics have wrestled with over the centuries, and indeed, that the history of Catholicism is a history of development of the understanding of these symbols. The proper method of understanding and interpreting the Bible, then, comes through being so steeped in its symbols and stories that the Bible somehow becomes the very language of wrestling with our modern problems. Scholarly investigation may help us understand the Bible, but it can never exhaust the meaning of the Biblical story. Every Catholic must seek to understand the Bible in order to be present to God who lives in its words. An awareness of His Biblical presence helps us find meaning in the events which seem to overwhelm us, bear with the evil that sometimes defeats us, and celebrate the mystery that invites us.

The Bible is the story of God and His relations with His people. It encourages certain attitudes and suggests certain behaviors, helping to shape the lives of individuals in the context of past interpretations of the Christian community. Written by human authors under the guidance of the Spirit, the Bible is a cumulative story in which different elements take on a powerful force due to tensions in culture and society. Though expressed in Jewish and Greek cultural categories, it presents not a limited exposition of ordinary events so much as a global vision of the world. It does not present an argument, nor a logical conceptual system, so much as a way of structuring insights that allows Christians to continue their quest for meaningful explanations of the world and personal existence.

Though the Bible is a collection of texts written by specific persons at specific times, its meaning is always more than the intent of the original authors. Though the scriptures are historically conditioned and contain the words of humans who acted and thought in the sociological context of their particular society, they contain a wonderful wealth of human diversity and pluralism. Those who approach the Bible to find meaning in their own lives have to understand that the Bible creates a Christian world view by structuring consciousness, encouraging attitudes, and suggesting behaviors. The reality of the scriptures consists not in trivial occurrences, but in the patterns of life. It entails, for example, care rather than apathy; concern for others rather than for self. The Bible must be responded to as a whole. The intricate interweaving of its story with one's personal experience becomes the individual's response to the "Word of God." The proper attitude in interpreting and responding to the word of God is to retain an openness to God's revelation.

Overview of the Bible

Roman Catholics are often overwhelmed with the sheer size of the Bible. Their confusion is compounded when they learn that Catholic and Protestant Bibles do not even contain the same books. Their sense of frustration continues when they learn that there have been dozens of translations through the centuries, each claiming to be more accurate than its predecessors. How can they make sense of all this confusion? Where should they begin?

disciples. These questions shaped the material of the accounts. The stories about Jesus that were most pertinent for their own lives determined what they remembered and collected. The words and deeds of Jesus were filtered through the selective memory of the disciples before they came to be written as the Christian scriptures. Various interpretations of the Christian message were developed by and for the Christian communities. From the several versions that were written and circulated, four became standard for the early community. They were called the four gospels.

The four gospels have a place of honor in the Christian community, much like the fundamental documents of freedom -- the Declaration of Independence, the Constitution, and the Bill of Rights -- have in the eyes of Americans. They have a special place because they are the charter of the new community, the proclamation of the "Good News" of salvation. None of the four gospels is a firsthand account of Jesus' public ministry. Each of the gospel authors (or editors), working from the remembrances of the early community, brings a creative approach to his portrait of Jesus. The four gospels present, under the guidance of the Spirit, not four biographies of Jesus, but different versions of how the early community understood their lives were changed by what God had done in Jesus. Each gospel describes in a different way how the human situation has been changed, how the threat of problems such as suffering, loneliness, and death are tempered in the light of the Resurrection of Jesus.

Mark's gospel, generally acknowledged to be the first one written, reads much like a police report, providing just bare facts and a minimum of interpretation. Like a local news program on television, it includes stories with specific eyewitness details, for example, the storm on the Sea of Galilee. Yet it is sometimes sketchy in its overall presentation, providing very few of the parables and sermons of Jesus and no details of His resurrection appearances. Probably written for the community of Christians living in

Rome, Mark's gospel leads to the central question "who do you say I am?" The answer, developed throughout the second half of the gospel, is a surprise, to say the least: Jesus is the Christ, or Messiah, yes, but a Messiah who has to suffer and who calls for discipleship at high cost from His followers. The Messiah, yes, but a Messiah whose mission is misunderstood (and thus kept hidden throughout the gospel). In Mark's portrait, Jesus is a very lonely person who nevertheless embraces the tragedies of life with confidence.

Matthew's gospel is placed first in the New Testament because it was written to Christians who had previously been Jews. It showed them that Jesus was the royal Messiah that had been promised to them. Matthew presents Jesus as the fulfillment of the Old Testament prophecies about the Messiah. He portrays Jesus as a lawgiver, like Moses, who not only interprets the law but brings it to fulfillment. This gospel might remind some persons of the recipes in a cookbook which use numbers as a guide. For example, Jesus' infancy narrative is described in five episodes and the Sermon on the Mount contains five statements about the observance of the law. In Matthew's portrait, Jesus is sent to teach others about the kingdom of God and promises guidance to those who follow His lifestyle in the structured community of the Church.

Luke's gospel might remind us of a gentle family doctor or soft-spoken lawyer, presenting Jesus' message of compassion, forgiveness, and concern for the plight of the poor and oppressed. Luke underscores the importance of prayer and the joy that comes in the Holy Spirit. He presents Jesus as the center of a grand scheme of salvation history. In the light of the Acts of the Apostles, Luke's companion piece to his gospel, Jesus is shown as the model for what God is doing and has done and for what the community is called to continue to do. In Luke's polished portrait for a Greek-speaking audience, Jesus proclaims the joy that comes through realizing the Father's forgiveness, that is, through sharing His mercy and care in the forgiveness of others.

John's gospel is the most difficult to understand, more mystical in orientation, much like reading a play of Eugene O'Neill or watching a movie of Ingmar Bergman. John writes for all Christians in a manner unlike that of the first three gospels. Reflecting on the meaning of the revelation of God in Jesus, John writes so that all Christians may go on believing in Christ as the Way, the Life, the Light, and the Truth. Whereas the purpose of the miracles in the Synoptic gospels is to evoke wonder in Jesus' power (Mark), call for faith (Matthew), or joy (Luke), the few miracles which John records have a symbolic context. They provide a setting for explaining his teaching which had been misunderstood by the disciples. John's gospel portrays Jesus as the one in whom eternal life has begun. He is the one who dies, confident that He will return to the Father, enter into His glory, and send His Spirit to be present in the community.

Resurrection as Revelation

From even such a brief consideration of each of the gospel writers it is evident that there are many understandings and interpretations of the meaning of the life of Jesus in the New Testament. Still, a large number of Catholics are reluctant to regard the gospel narratives as anything other than straight historical reporting of the life of Jesus. In fact, however, the gospels present that life -- His words and deeds -- as colored by the resurrection. They present a variety of ways that Jesus, as the revelation of God, is still present in the Christian community.

When His followers proclaimed that "Jesus is risen indeed" they were not claiming that He returned in His physical body. Nor did they mean merely that He was spiritually present, as for example, some persons could be said to live on in their descendants or their writings. To profess that "Jesus is risen indeed" meant that an historical person, a human like themselves, was given a new life after death. The Good News was that now all humans had the possibility of such a life in this life. The resurrection of

Jesus was understood as a stamp of approval by God the Father for Jesus' lifestyle of service to others. By striving to follow the lead of Jesus -- transforming the world by proclaiming liberty to captives, recovery of sight to the blind, and justice for the poor and oppressed -- they could also make present the activity of God just as Jesus had done.

This insight, which was made clear by the real presence of the risen Jesus, restructured the worldview of the disciples. The real presnce of Jesus in the resurrection was the signal of their own potential for new existence, for their own divinization. By manifesting the real presence of God in their own lives, as Jesus did, they helped bring about that kingdom of peace, that reign of ultimate human happiness in union with God, which Jesus preached. Perhaps by seeing the profound effect of the real presence of the risen Jesus in some of the early followers of Jesus, we may better understand the multiple ways that God chooses to reveal Himself in the Christian community. Let us see the transformation brought about by the resurrection in the lives of Mary Magdalene, Thomas, Peter, and the two disciples who were returning to their home village of Emmaus after the crucifixion in Jerusalem.

Magdalene: Presence Through Touch

Magdalene was the first to see Jesus after His death (cf. John 20: 1-2, 11-18). It is through her that John and Peter and the other apostles hear the Good News that the body is no longer in the tomb. Magdalene, a woman, is the first bearer of the Good News of the resurrection. Standing outside the empty tomb, Magdalene asks a person she presumes to be a gardener where the body of Jesus has been taken. In the recognition scene that follows, the "gardener," who turns out to be Jesus himself, tells Magdalene not to cling to His body but to go to the disciples and tell them that He is ascending. Running to the disciples with the Good News, she proclaims that she has seen the Lord.

The Magdalene episode shows that Jesus has been

transformed by the resurrection. He is going to the Father in order to send His Spirit to humanity. His presence henceforth will be through the Spirit. Magdalene's mistake in taking Him for a gardener not only points out the transformation of Jesus, but also her own transformation. She, too, has to undergo a change. She is told not to cling to Him; not to hold onto the Jesus she had known, but to hold onto Him who has overcome death through resurrection.

Magdalene recognizes that the permanent presence of Jesus is not through the physical appearance which she could touch but through the Spirit who is present spiritually. Henceforth, she and the other disciples are to "touch" others with the Good News: they are to live the resurrection in their lives and in so doing touch the lives of others. Magdalene's mission in coming to the tomb had been to annoint the body. Once she experienced the risen Jesus, she leaves with the mission to touch the lives of others by proclaiming the continued presence of Jesus.

By recognizing Jesus in the person of the gardener, she proclaims that we should see people in a different way. No longer are individuals merely gardeners, plumbers, cable TV repairmen, or whatever; they are now real encounters with Jesus who is present in His Spirit, Jesus whose body is somehow different than before, not recognized on sight or touch. Magdalene provides a model for the way that we are called to "touch" others. Everyday activity -- winks, grins, conscious awareness of another's presence -- can all be occasions for making the risen Jesus really present. Those moments when the lives of others are touched by evoking the real presence of Jesus now become moments when God reveals Himself to humanity.

Thomas: Presence Through Faith

Thomas is another person who provides a Biblical insight into the real presence of Jesus. Thomas is not at the gathering of the apostles when Jesus appears, so he does not hear Jesus proclaim peace, commission the apostles to experience the Spirit, and bring forgiveness to others (John 20: 19-29). Thomas, doubting, refuses to believe that Jesus is risen till he has touched and seen Him. The following week Jesus once again takes the initiative and manifests His presence. This time Thomas is in the group. Jesus announces that all those people are happy who have found faith in Him even though they have not been privileged to see and touch His risen body. Though Thomas laid down defiant conditions for overcoming his doubts, refused to accept the word of others, and insisted on the miraculous aspect of Jesus' presence, his significance in the early Church was in his faith commitment ("My Lord and my God") when he does encounter the risen Jesus.

Too many persons want to be shown the physical Jesus before they will believe in His real presence. Yet, even in the resurrection stories, seeing by itself is not always enough for recognition. Rather than berating Thomas for wanting to see and touch Jesus, we should appreciate him for allowing us to see Jesus in a different light. Because Thomas doubts, Jesus asks us to shift our emphasis from a physical, visible demonstration of His bodily presence to the recognition of His ongoing activity in the Spirit. His doubt shows that the demand for a visible proof is a betrayal of a narrow vision and lack of understanding of the meaning of the resurrection. It is a demand that Jesus return to His former physical state in order to be present to us. By seeing and recognizing the risen Jesus, Thomas gives us a new insight into reality that is both spiritual and'physical. By his demand for a rigid physical test for Jesus' presence, Thomas shows it is possible for others to make that faith commitment which enables them to see a lot more than meets the eye. He enables us to see that Jesus is present today not so much because we want Him to be, but because Jesus himself takes the initiative and makes a gift of His presence.

Once Thomas sees the risen Jesus and proclaims his faith, his life has a new focal point. Thomas provides us with a new way of seeing time. For example, those who are able to grasp the real presence

of Jesus in faith and not only through physical
presence have a new hindsight and foresight. By
their faith they are now free to draw support from the
past and maintain their situation in the present,
while always striving toward a new future. Time becomes pregnant with the consciousness of their own
divine destiny. Their insight cushions them against
future shock by keeping them continually open to the
spontaneous and changeable. Thanks to Thomas' experience of the real presence of Jesus in the resurrection,
we now see ourselves as living in the perspective of
the end-time, able to avoid depression or resignation
in the face of sad moments or death-dealing blows
because we recognize we are moving toward a future
where God will be all in all.

Peter: Presence Through Forgiveness

Peter's role in the resurrection stories provides
another insight into Jesus' real presence. While all
the apostles are accorded a share in the missionary
charge to proclaim the Good News, Peter is given the
place of prominence. Of the many resurrection stories
in the Bible concerning Peter's authority in the early
Christian community, one of the most revealing is the
episode in John (Jn 21: 1-17). In this story Peter
is forgiven by Jesus and given the mission to "feed
the lambs and feed the sheep" and, like a shepherd,
to lay down his life for his flock.

After a breakfast of fish and bread, which he
prepares for the apostles who have spent the night
fishing in vain, Jesus asks Peter three times if he
loves Him. Each time Peter proclaims his love for
Jesus, and each time he is told to "feed the sheep."
This threefold affirmation of love is a reversal of
Peter's earlier threefold denial of Jesus. The scene
is a rehabilitation scene, an act of forgiveness on
the part of Jesus. This rehabilitation is the basis
for Peter's authority and mission in the early community. Precisely, because Peter has been guilty of
not following his master, indeed guilty of denying
Him, he is the first recipient of the forgiveness of
the risen Jesus. Peter's role in the early Church
is to forgive, precisely because he knows most what

it means to be forgiven. Though Jesus prayed that Peter's faith would not fail, he forgives him when it does fail. This forgiveness strengthens Peter's mission: from now on he is to show a solicitude for others similar to the solicitude that Jesus has shown him. Peter is now to seek out and forgive those who have gone astray and bring them back to the flock.

Peter becomes a "wounded healer." When denying Jesus, he was spiritually sick, but now Jesus' forgiveness cures him. Now he can bring this same healing to others. By acknowledging the suffering and sickness in his own heart, he can more easily recognize and forgive it in others. After the resurrection, Peter becomes the representative of Jesus as the symbol of God's forgiveness to all people: Jesus is really present in the act of forgiveness. Peter's experience of being forgiven and his power to forgive others are not due to any personal merit on his part, but solely to the free gift of the risen Jesus.

Peter receives this gift, called a "charism," which entails the responsibility of making forgiveness a reality in the Christian community. He has the mission to proclaim forgiveness, for he has been forgiven. Now Peter is to "re-present," make Jesus' presence real in the community. Peter is the foundation stone, the "rock" of the community of forgiveness.

The forgiveness Peter experienced is a radical reorientation of his personality. He is the model of the experience of forgiveness, and forgiving, for all Catholics. Forgiveness is one evident unifying experience of God and humanity. When one person is able to forgive another, where there is mutual recognition of guilt and forgiveness, there is also an occasion for the real presence of the risen Jesus. The Catholic Church is the community of those who are aware of this forgiveness and the continual need for it. The recognition that we have been forgiven and that we still need to be forgiven is an eschatological element of the Church. Such an awareness of forgiveness is an experience of the risen Lord, and an anticipation of the victory of the coming kingdom. He is made present each

time the members of the Christian community experience
the healing power of forgiveness by forgiving or being
forgiven.

Emmaus: Presence in Eucharist

One last resurrection appearance shows another of
God's revealing presences. Two disciples were returning to the small village of Emmaus, not far from
Jerusalem, after the crucifixion and death of Jesus
(Lk 24: 13-35). Sadness and discouragement veiled
their hearts. Jesus' ministry had enkindled their
hopes and expectations of a Messiah who would restore
the kingdom of David, yet his death shattered these
hopes. They thought this kingdom would become a
reality in this life. Then a stranger encounters
them along the road. It is Jesus, who accompanies
them without disclosing His identity. He joins them
while they talk of Him. He is present, but they
think Him far away. Programmed to experience the
presence of Jesus only as he had been physically
present to them during His lifetime, they are prevented
from understanding Jesus as He unfolds the meaning of
the scriptures to them.

Not until their arrival at an inn at the out-
skirts of Emmaus do they recognize who the stranger
really is. Only when Jesus explains the scriptures
and shares bread with them are they aware of the
presence of the risen Jesus. Their despair and disap-
pointment overcome, they are filled with joy and
hasten back to proclaim the Good News to the others
in Jerusalem. Because these two disciples heard the
words of the Bible and shared a meal with a stranger,
they undergo a radical conversion and become enthused
to share this inner change with others.

Their new awareness comes from a new understanding
of the Bible, but the understanding happens in the
context of a meal. Once again, the mere physical
presence of Jesus is not enough to bring someone to
believe in the real presence of the risen Jesus. Only
gradually do they realize that the real presence is
not limited to His physical body. They can then

bequeath a legacy to all Christians. Though it is not possible for all of us today to encounter the risen Jesus, we can encounter His real presence in the Bible and in the sacramental meal.

The Good News that the Emmaus disciples bring back to the apostles is that the stranger they met on the way is really the risen Jesus. Their receptiveness to a stranger gradually gives them a new outlook on themselves and their mission. The stranger forces them to admit that their previous world view was inadequate and to acknowledge that their way of life and hopes for a worldly kingdom were not enough. Their response to the stranger, and their hospitality in inviting him to share a dinner with them leads to unexpected joys.

The Emmaus disciples provide us with a model for our own faith-response. Such a response allows strangers to be themselves and not be reduced to extensions or projections of others. Strangers are allowed to summon us to an encounter with the unknown, with the unexpected, with the "thief in the night." Strangers enable Jesus to be present even in His absence. In strangers Jesus surprises us and reveals what each unique person can become, having been created in the divine image. In strangers Jesus can be the source of self-knowledge, challenging us to respond to God's self-revelation and to commit ourselves to the action of bringing the Good News to others. Such a commitment retains its enthusiasm and life-giving power insofar as it is refreshed by hearing the Word of God and sharing the bread.

Conclusion

God reveals Himself to us in many ways. Catholics believe that there is a uniqueness in the way God makes His presence known, such that it can be shared by many. This revelation of God occurs in the community of the Church through the continuing presence of Jesus, the definitive revelation of the Father. Since the event of the resurrection this presence of Jesus is through the Holy Spirit. It is real even though it is not self-evident. Though Catholics have tended to stress the real presence of Jesus in the Eucharist, as a reaction against the Protestant insistence on the revelation of God in the word of the Bible, they have lately begun to appreciate other parts of their heritage.

In this chapter we examined the real presence of Jesus in the Bible. We found there clues to other ways in which God reveals Himself. While Catholics have always sensed an experience of contact with God in their beliefs, rituals, and ethical actions, they can learn from the stories surrounding the resurrection appearances of other ways in which God reveals Himself to humanity. The revelation of God, which we have referred to as the real presence of Jesus, is manifested to the community of believers: when, like Magdalene, they touch the lives of others by their care and solicitude; when it comes alive through a Thomas-like faith in a vision of the coming kingdom, where God will be all in all; when it is present in the forgiveness of a Peter. Finally, the revelation of God comes through listening to the strangers we meet along the way, as the Emmaus disciples did, who show new insights into the real presence of Jesus whenever the word of God is heard and the Bread shared.

QUESTIONS

Personal Reflection

1. Have you ever felt God's presence? Where? When? Were you alone? Was it similar to any other feeling you ever had?

2. Get a copy of the Bible. Read in it the first chapter of the Old Testament; the first chapter of each gospel. Have you ever heard this material before? Which first chapter do you like best?

3. Which of the descriptions of Jesus in the gospels do you like most?

4. Which of the presences of Jesus do you like most?

5. Is there anything you can do to make His presence more real? Do you want to do it?

Group Discussion

1. Have you ever seen a movie or television show dealing with people who have experienced God? Is this the way most people experience God?

2. How important is the Bible to contemporary American life? To American life of the last century? Should the Bible assist us in making personal or national decisions? How?

3. Were the writers of the gospels true reporters if they did not agree upon details of Jesus' life?

4. Are the presences of Jesus found among people you know? Are there some presences which are never found?

5. If Jesus is present in so many ways, who is He? Is there a real Jesus or is He a figment of our imagination?

Review Questions

1. Describe personal presence and physical presence. Are they the same or different?

2. What does it mean to say that the Bible is the word of God?

3. What is revelation? How is resurrection revelation?

4. Describe the various effects of Jesus' real presence upon his followers.

5. What are the options of God's presence? Which way is God present in the two stories at the beginning of this chapter?

6. Describe the four gospels and how they each portray Jesus.

SUGGESTED READINGS

Brown, Raymond et al. (eds.)
<u>Jerome</u> <u>Biblical</u> <u>Commentary</u>
1969

80 articles by competent Roman Catholic scholars which present a compact and complete study of modern Biblical scholarship.

Brown, Raymond
<u>The</u> <u>Virginal</u> <u>Conception</u> and <u>Bodily</u> <u>Resurrection</u> <u>of</u> Jesus
Paulist, 1973

Use of Biblical criticism to survey and evaluate current challenges to the historicity of the stories surrounding Jesus' birth and resurrection.

Greeley, Andrew
<u>The</u> <u>Jesus</u> <u>Myth</u>
Doubleday, 1973

Review of some modern research on the person and teaching of Jesus, and an elaboration on the love and joy of his message.

Guzie, Tad
<u>Jesus</u> <u>and</u> <u>the</u> <u>Eucharist</u>
Paulist, 1974

A return to the idea of the presence of Christ as a way of symbolizing the connection between the action of Christians and the Lord whose victory they celebrate.

Juel, Donald
<u>An</u> <u>Introduction</u> <u>to</u> <u>New</u> <u>Testament</u> <u>Literature</u>
Abingdon, 1978

Clear and concise approach to the Bible using insights from literary criticism.

O'Collins, Gerald
<u>What</u> <u>are</u> <u>they</u> <u>Saying</u> <u>About</u> <u>the</u> <u>Resurrection?</u>
Paulist, 1978

Helpful overview of the weaknesses and strengths of current theological interpretations of the resurrection.

Perkins, Pheme
Reading the New Testament:
An Introduction
Paulist, 1978

A readable introduction to the New Testament using the latest developments of historico-critical study.

Perrin, Norman
The Resurrection According
to Matthew, Mark, and Luke
Fortress, 1977

An illuminating study of the three Synoptic accounts of the resurrection and a new understanding of the Easter celebration.

Topel, L. John
The Way to Peace: Liberation Through the Bible
Orbis, 1979

Systematic tracing of the roots of liberation theology in both the Old and New Testaments.

III. WORDS OF PEOPLE: OPTIONS OF FAITH

LEN BIALLAS

Recently I watched a Sunday Mass on television. The camera panned the people in the congregation while they recited the Nicene Creed. Here was a youngster saying "Jesus punches the pilot" and there an older person, perhaps hard of hearing, proclaiming, "the proceeds are from the Father and the Son." Still another person was fingering the beads of a rosary while ushers were busy in the back getting the collection baskets ready. This was truly the Catholic Church: the people shared a common faith in the Nicene Creed, yet they expressed that faith in their own individual ways.

Faith is a vague word and means different things to different people. Faith may be belief in God and going to Church on Sunday. It may be what we have in common with those who went to the same parochial school. Faith may be what a man and woman should share in order to get married in the Catholic Church. Perhaps all of these are part of faith, but none of them really captures the essence of faith.

Even the Church rituals show some of the confusion surrounding the word "faith." In the baptismal ceremony, for example, one of the first questions the priest asks is what a person desires from the Church. One of the options for response is "faith." This is strange, isn't it? A person would not present himself for baptism unless he already had some kind of faith. So what is really happening? Individuals bring one kind of faith to the Church, and the Church shares another kind with them. One type of faith, the shared symbol-life of the Catholic community, formulated in its creeds and traditions, is more objective. These were called constitutive elements in the first chapter. The other, the individual's response and openness to the call and activity of God, is more subjective.

For the purposes of this chapter on the options
of faith I would like to clarify what I mean by
"faith" by contrasting it with "belief" and "doctrine."
It should be noted that the distinctions I am making
are not universally recognized, and many continue to
use all three words -- belief, doctrine, and faith --
interchangeably.

1) Belief is the broadest of the three terms, desig-
nating a trust or confidence, a judgment or mental
acceptance of something as true, even though absolute
certainty may be absent. 2) Doctrine is belief insofar as it is a synthesis of Catholic thought. Doctrine
refers to the teaching of the Church, a carefully
worked-out system which is taught, advocated, and
handed down from one generation to another. To the
extent that this is handed down by the Church authorities as true and indisputable, it is sometimes called
"dogma," or even, confusingly, "the faith." Doctrine
remains unchanging throughout the centuries. 3) Faith
is unquestioning belief that does not require proof
or evidence. It is an assent to God, moved by love.
Faith is personal acceptance of and response to the
unchanging objective doctrines of the Church. As a
subjective response, faith changes as individuals
in each generation respond differently due to the
peculiarities of their culture.

Doctrine and faith, then, are two different forms
of belief. One refers to what is believed -- the
objective teachings of the Church -- and the other
refers to how it is believed -- the subjective response
and personal commitment to God. In this chapter I
want to trace some of the different options of the
second type of belief -- personal faith -- which are
current among Catholics. Before doing so, however, it
will be useful to look at belief as doctrine and belief
as faith in more detail.

Belief As Doctrine

Belief as doctrine is a system of propositions
for explaining reality, a synthesis of Catholic thought.
Doctrine means the truths necessary for salvation,

not given by the light of natural reason, but of which
the Church is the custodian and dispenser. From the
time of the Reformation in the 16th century, to be a
"true" Catholic meant to acknowledge the doctrines of
the Church and to subscribe to a list of articles.
Doctrine is a system of explaining reality that is
closed and distinct from other religious systems.
It provides a point of absolute reference, a vision
of the world distinct from all other religions. One's
doctrine enables one to distinguish "true" from "false"
teachings. It gives the Catholic community a sense of
identity in truth and separation from falsehood.

It is striking how few doctrines of the Catholic
Church there are. The character and heritage of the
Catholic Church is expressed not only in its doctrines
but also in its scriptures, ethical systems, rituals,
and religious experiences. Doctrines constitute only
a small part of Catholic life and activity, and most
of the basic ones have come down to us unchanged from
the first general councils of the Church. In common
with other religions, Catholic doctrines are concerned
with a few fundamental questions. All religions have
doctrines about God: whether God is personal, eternal,
loving, and separate from or involved in the history
of the world. All religions make statements about
humanity: origin, nature, and destiny. Finally, all
religions answer questions about the world: is it
created or not, real or merely an illusion, eternal
or not, basically good or evil? In all three of these
areas -- God, humanity, and the world -- the uniqueness
of Catholic doctrine has as its essential ingredient
the person, mission, and continued presence of Jesus.

At the heart of Catholic doctrine is Jesus, the
God-man. In and through Jesus, Catholics learn what
God is, what humans are, and where salvation lies.
Catholics believe that Jesus is the person in whom the
goal of all humanity has been fully revealed. In
Jesus God is revealed as a parent who loves humanity --
His children -- so much that he wishes to share His own
life with all of them. Humans have this spark of
divine life, an absolutely free gift, through their
association with the Catholic Church of which Jesus

is the head. Their salvation, anticipated in those
acts which imitate the ministry of Jesus in loving,
forgiving, caring for, and serving others, is their
reunion or communion with God. This core of Catholic
doctrine is a systematic reflection on what Catholics
hear in the gospel narratives. Doctrines proclaim
in philosophical language the significance and meaning
of the birth of Jesus (the Incarnation) and the end of
His life (death and resurrection) for the salvation
of humanity.

Many items in the Catholic heritage and practice
are not matters of doctrine, but rather elements of
cultural, political, and historical development.
There are many areas where doubts are in no way reflections or denials of the Catholic tradition. For
example, whether it is suitable for a priest to celebrate Mass facing the congregation and in English,
whether Adam and Eve really existed, whether divine
providence means that God actually sends sickness and
accidents to people, and whether Jesus knew from the
moment of His birth about His mission as the Christ
are all matters of opinion, not doctrine.

The elements of Catholic doctrine represent
layers of refinement of the essential doctrine of the
God-man Jesus through the centuries. Such refinement
was due to cultural, devotional, and political factors.
Doctrines about the humanity and divinity of Jesus,
about the Trinity, about creation, redemption, and
grace, for example, were developed early as elaborations
within a cultural context on the gift of salvation that
God had made available through Jesus. Personal devotions and piety were instrumental in further refining
the core of doctrine in the proclamation of the real
presence of Jesus in the Eucharist and, later, in the
amplifications on the role and destiny of Mary, His
mother. Politics played a role in developing an understanding of the presence of the Spirit of Jesus in His
Church and in the doctrine of papal infallibility.
Not all of these doctrines are equal in importance;
and assent, though necessary for all Catholics, is
expressed in individual ways in the lifestyle of each
person.

As an essential part of the heritage of the Catholic tradition, doctrines have several positive aspects. Doctrines provide a common bond of unity with Catholics over the centuries, bring vitality to the community, and furnish order and focus for individual experiences.

Doctrines, first of all, unite Catholics with each other and with their heritage of past generations. They give legitimate unity to the expression of faith which is required of all Catholics by providing a common language and vehicle for reciprocal communication. Along with the other parts of the Catholic heritage, such as the lives of the saints, prayers, and ritual practices, doctrines deepen the roots of Catholicism found in the Gospels and build a sense of community through many generations.

Catholic doctrines are part of the long history of rereading, rewriting, and reinterpreting the Word of God in the Bible in the attempt to relate this Word to present time and present needs. The scriptures are the Word of God under the inspiration of the Holy Spirit; the doctrines are the Spirit-directed reflections upon that written Word by the believing Church over the centuries. Doctrines are formulations in a philosophical language which spell out the content of the Gospel story in such a way as to be relevant for succeeding generations. They are the logical explanation and distillation of what is already present in scripture for different cultures and succeeding historical situations. As an integral part of the life of the liturgy and discipleship, doctrines create and safeguard the unity of the Catholic Church through the adoption of common and clear expressions.

Secondly, doctrines bring vitality to the Catholic community by revealing the presence of Christ in the Church and in the world. Using a conceptual framework, doctrines provide a better understanding of the person, function, and message of Jesus. Doctrines do not constitute an archaeological museum or dead depository, but come alive as an organism in the hearts, minds, and actions of each generation of the Church. As the

71

symbolic response of the community's experiences of belief and hope and action, they are the vital energy that Catholics draw on to aid them in their response to God's invitation to share the divine life.

Thirdly, doctrines bring order and meaning to individual experiences. They are the deliberate affirmation of what Catholics consider of unrestricted value and ultimate concern. They focus on the very center of Catholic life in the assertion of the gratuitous gift of love that God has disclosed to humanity in Jesus and made present in the ongoing life of the Church. Through their rich symbolic structure, doctrines enable those who experience the life of the Catholic community to have a basic pattern for interpreting and evaluating life. Actions are not performed meaninglessly, but in the light of the realization that they are the working out of each person's share in God's own life.

Belief as Faith

The subjective side of belief -- faith -- is far more than intellectual acceptance of the doctrines of the Church. It is a loyal adherence to a personal God, a state of consciousness which results from coming into relationship with the divine reality. A person is seized deeply in the heart by God and acts accordingly. Though faith contains an element of trust, it is not a blind belief which destroys intellectual honesty. The Church Fathers at Vatican II suggest that faith is the obedience given to God who reveals, an obedience by which a person entrusts the whole self freely to God, freely assenting to the truth revealed by Him (Rev. art. 5). Faith is an individual's active participation, due to the grace of God and the interior help of the Holy Spirit, in finding one's full potential as a human being.

Faith is saying "yes" to life. Yet life changes. Children, for example, experience almost the entire world as the unknown. Wonder or fear may be provoked by any real or imagined reality. Faith at this stage is saying "yes" to God's world and one's life in it.

Adolescents, on the other hand, face the unknown in their budding sexuality. The move from consciousness of sexuality to a consent to intimacy and its concomitant responsibilities is a daring venture. Faith at this stage is saying "yes" to God's invitation to love others as He loved us. Adults experience the unknown under the guise of their mortality. Confidence and clarity in the face of one's own certain death are not easily achieved. Faith at this final stage of life is saying "yes" to God's gift of a share in His divine life.

Faith commitment is expressed in different ways at different stages of life, yet many persons seem reluctant to move beyond the childlike faith that is expressed in a vague belief in God as the creator of the universe. They justify their hesitation to move to an adult faith commitment in many ways. Thus, for example, they might say that a profession of faith, without personal involvement, is sufficient for salvation. Or they might claim that doctrines are noble and irrelevant monuments to the past which hinder the immediate experience of the Holy Spirit today. Still others might suggest that doctrines are slogan summaries, not susceptible to historical proof or demonstration, not immediately understood or elaborated, and thus not be be taken seriously lest they falsify rather than clarify the appeal of the Good News. Most of these rationalizations stem from the idea that faith is merely an assent to the propositions of doctrine rather than an entire lifestyle.

Faith commitment cannot be logically demonstrated, but only invited, encouraged, and supported. The Catholic Church community, through its rituals and other religious experiences, is the primary force in the process of forming those visions, judgments, and decision-making habits which constitute faith. Individual believers provide additional support by the personal witness of their own involvement in building up God's kingdom through such activities as social justice movements and those healing relationships which separate people. Theologians, too, function to make the doctrines of the Church relevant for each generation so that each individual Catholic is drawn to make the faith commitment.

Theologians as Mediators

Faith is a living, growing, dynamic personal response to the call of God. Assent to the propositions in the Catholic doctrines is one ingredient of this faith, an essential but not sufficient ingredient. While the bishops of the Church have the responsibility for preserving the unity of doctrine in the Church, the theologians function to vitalize personal faith by helping Catholics understand these doctrines in a plurality of ways. The bishops' role is to preserve the substance of doctrine; the theologian's role to promote different formulations of faith. Bishops affirm the unchanging truth of doctrine; theologians provide evolving representations of it in such a way that the Church continues to be a living reality in the world. A person can be both theologian and bishop.

In a way, theologians are mediators between the two kinds of belief, between doctrine and faith. They seek to preserve the life, vision, and ideals of the common heritage by probing the orientation and background of the doctrines and then attempting new formulations of them so that individuals may appropriate them more easily into their own personal faith. In fidelity to the proclamation of Jesus, to the earliest layers of apostolic tradition, to the Church fathers and Church Councils, theologians stress different interpretations which they hope will strike a responsive chord in their particular historical and cultural situation. To do this they make use of the concepts, terms, and images typical of the intellectual climate of their time. They attempt to formulate the common heritage in a way that maintains authentic continuity with the past and is still suitable for Catholic living in the present, but may be inadequate for future ages.

While retaining the centrality of Jesus' vision of life, theologians attempt to discern how the revelation of God's grace and love in Jesus changes scope as new courses of action are presented and new problems and obstacles faced. Genuine theologians

are not changing the doctrine of Catholicism. They
are pointing out the continually unfolding implications
for personal responses or options of faith. Jesus and
His ministry of loving, caring, forgiving, and serving
remain the basic route of access to the abundant and
eternal life of the Kingdom. Still, each generation
has to realize this call to salvation in its own way.
Theologians serve the Catholic Church in delineating
a worldview that incorporates new ranges of alterna-
tives, new sets of unasked questions, and new avenues
of exploration which stem directly from the unchanging
doctrine of the Catholic heritage.

How Catholics become involved in the story of
Jesus is not as decisive as the fact that they understand their lives as a response to God's love. A
glance at five of the faith options currently popular
among theologians show the richness of this Catholic
heritage. These options are, in turn, redemption,
liberation, process, story, and encounter with world
religions.

None of these options is peculiarly Catholic,
except perhaps in the stress on Jesus as mediator
and the strong insistence on the role of individuals
in co-creating their own future. Indeed, it is difficult to find any theology today that is exclusively
Catholic. All five options claim that Jesus is an
essential part of the strategy of the faith response
to the doctrines of the Church. They all presume that
Catholicism is rooted in an interpersonal relationship.
The partners in this relationship are, on one hand,
God and Jesus, who has proclaimed the Good News of a
share in the divine life, and on the other hand,
Catholics who have been transformed due to the power
of the Spirit.

Each of the five options of faith consists of
three parts: a problem, a strategy, and a solution.
First, there is the problem to be overcome (for example, social injustice, meaninglessness, or alienation),
a roadblock confronting life's genuine satisfactions
which must be removed before life can realize its
goals. Second, there is the strategy, an effective
means of action that can transform people to help them

overcome the problem. Jesus provides the model for
this strategy, for example, in His commitment to the
Kingdom, His sense of union with the Father, or His
psychological wholeness. Finally, there is the
solution of the problem, the goal, realizable in life
(for example, a liberation, a grace-experience, a
sharing in the resurrection), that Catholics strive
for. To live in opposition to this solution is to
have bad faith, to have inauthentic existence, to sin.
Books have been written about each of the options in
which a full vision of the Catholic life is developed.
We will merely provide a brief sketch of each one.

Redemption

The first option might be called classical, traditional, or conservative. It has been a major theological preoccupation since the time of Augustine in the
5th century, if not before. It formed part of the
medieval background of Anselm's development of a system
of atonement and satisfaction. From this perspective
the history of the world forms part of a process of
salvation history. In language reminiscent of the law
courts, Christ came to redeem humanity because of
Adam's sin. The Catholic's appropriate response is
gratitude to the redeemer and an ascetic distance
from the world, which is "a valley of tears."

The problem is that human nature is fractured,
fallen, and corrupt. Humanity is perversion, manifested in the original sin of Adam and Eve and passed
from one generation to the next. The environment we
live in is hostile and is the result, not the cause,
of our corruption. Evil is personified in the devil
who rules the world through his principalities and
powers. The devil makes human pleasure the end to
which all of life's processes minister and makes
human perceptions the norms by which all things are
to be judged. Human nature, in a word, conforms to
a godless world and needs redemption.

The strategy is based on a supernaturalistic
world view. The main idea is that God, in the person
of His son, broke into our space-time world. Jesus
is the new Adam who redeems humanity by buying us out

76

f slavery to Satan. Through His life and death Jesus
ecures forgiveness for all. This forgiveness is due
olely to God's grace, for God takes the initiative
n salvation and makes it available to those who,
hrough baptism, have been initiated into the Roman
atholic Church.

The strategy, as it applies to individual Catho-
ics, is to be renewed and indwelt by the Holy Spirit.
t means accepting God's forgiveness through imitation
f Christ in His life and death. This is realized
y a lifetime of obedience to Church teaching and by
ourishment through the Church's sacraments. Catholics
re to exercise the virtues of faith, hope, and love,
hile they wait with patience for the glory that is to
ome. They are members of a pilgrim church, moving
teadily to the final age at the end of the world.

The solution is a transfiguration or diviniza-
ion, in the end, a new relationship to God. The goal
s to see God in His unveiled glory in the beatific
ision. It is a salvation primarily in the future,
eing with Christ, being ushered into His life, aban-
oning forever the final vestiges of sin, and receiving
 new resurrection body. Catholics long for the full
erfection to be attained only in the glory of heaven,
hen the time comes for the restoration of all things,
erfectly reestablished in Christ. Catholics look for-
rd to the day when the Lord will come in majesty and
l His angels with Him, when death will be destroyed
d all things will be subject to Him.

In a sense the other four theological options for
aith are a foil to the traditional view. They are
lternative visions to the fall/redemption tradition.

iberation

"Liberation" theology is the second of the five
ptions. Emerging out of the social encyclicals and
heologies of hope, revolution, or politics, libera-
ion theology attacks the social oppression of the
uffering masses. It deals with the struggle and
rowth of consciousness that must occur to liberate

the oppressed. All those who suffer injustice -- the poor, blacks, women, native Americans -- are subjects for thought and action. A common expression of this theology is found among Catholic theologians in Latin America. Two typical representatives of this school are Jon Sobrino and Gustavo Gutierrez.

The problem according to liberation theology is any established order, law, or value-system which oppresses or represses society; any social institution which overwhelms individuals and keeps them from making truly human responses is the oppressor. It is any social structure which presents obstacles to living as fully human beings, making both the oppressors and the oppressed act out of hostility rather than love, in-difference rather than concern, individualism rather than a sense of community. Whether it goes by the name of poverty, oppression, or prejudice, and whether it is considered a bondage to sin, transience, or death, it must be overcome. It is a demonic power from which the consciousness of the oppressed must first be liberated and then utilized to transform and humanize political, economic, and social structures.

The strategy consists in following the lifestyle of Jesus as the one who "pulled the powerful from their thrones and exalted the lowly, the one who sent the rich away empty and filled the poor with good things" (Luke 1: 52-53). The mission of Jesus was to care for the outcasts, the poor, and the sinners. His ministry was to bring them peace by proclaiming that all persons were loveable, even in their strug-gles. He taught that humanity's responsibility to God and others was not exercised in strict observance of the law, but through being seized by the love of the Father. Indeed, His death, His total gift of self, was the response par excellence to the Father's love. For this response He was vindicated by God who raised Him from the dead and sent His Spirit among His followers.

For the individual Catholic this strategy con-sists in becoming aware of and rooted in the indwelling presence of the Spirit of Jesus. It means seeing

78

one's actions as a response to the divine initiative, as an attempt to build up God's Kingdom through any activity where the poor and exploited are helped to overcome their oppression. Examples of such activities are the activities of Friendship House, the Catholic Worker Movement, and participation in protests for civil rights. Liberation theology finds its justification in action. Marginal existence is sometimes called for, since affluence and institutional comfort are usually incompatible with liberation spirituality, and are all too often short cuts leading to a human wasteland, not to the Kingdom. Courage, not comfort, is the pivotal means to obtain leverage to overthrow unjust situations.

The solution or goal in this theological option is the Kingdom of God seen as an experience of both internal and external liberation. Internally, it means an awareness of the vital surge of God's Spirit which is transforming human existence and enabling the community to participate and create its own history rather than be formed by someone else's history. Externally, the goal is salvation through a people, a fellowship, a common effort to create a better order. The goal is a new world, created wherever persons heal wounds, overcome social injustice, and bring about reconciliation. It is a world not awaited passively, but anticipated and realized wherever human institutions are restructured so that all individuals are free to develop their full personalities in the image of God. This is the realization of the Kingdom that Jesus preached, here and now, wherever the needs of others are cared for. In Biblical terms, this liberation from injustice and hatred is often referred to as "salvation from sin."

Process-Evolution

A third option which helps some people formulate a faith response may be called "process" or "evolutionary" theology. Those who work out of this framework usually acknowledge either the philosopher, Alfred Whitehead, or the theologian-paleontologist, Teilhard de Chardin, as a source of their ideas. The

central thesis is that evolution, despite its many
blind alleys, is a process with an upward ascent,
marked with an ever-increasing development of the
human person. From this perspective the universe is
a constellation of events, or processes, which are
interrelated and interlocking. Each event is part of
a dynamic forward movement, a becoming in which the
past is summed up, the present accomplished, and the
future shaped.

The problem according to process or evolutionary
theology is the mentality that sees change, passage,
or temporality as evil. As applied to persons, such
a mentality assumes that humans are disunited and
divided between their material and spiritual selves,
their "flesh" and their "spirit." Humans will always
be necessarily imperfect because they are juxtaposi-
tions of body, which is changing and therefore evil,
and soul, which is unchanging and therefore good.
Applied to God, this mentality shuns the deep para-
doxes which arise from the limitations of human per-
ception when it tries to grasp the mystery and majesty
of God. It assumes that God is infinite and unchanging, aloof and in no way related to what goes on in
His creation, ruling people in a tyrannical fashion
and answering prayers at His whim. The problem with
this mentality is that a false dichotomy is set up
between this world and the next, between this "valley
of tears" and our "true home in heaven."

The strategy consists in perceiving Jesus as the
one whose divinity consisted in the perfection of His
humanity. True God and true man, His human nature
was the actualization of human reality. Through Him
divinity and humanity interpenetrated each other in
love. The embodiment of outgoing, active, and creative
goodness, Jesus was the person who incarnated love to
such an extent that people believed that God had visited them in Him. Jesus was radically different for in
Him humanity crossed a new critical threshold in the
evolutionary process; in Him possibilities open to
human nature became capable of realization. Jesus
marked the unique leap from the lower level of matter
toward a higher spiritual unity, or more precisely,

Jesus revealed the spiritual dimension of matter.
Jesus manifested the fullest potential of the God-man
relationship and thus made it accessible to all persons. By revealing God as present in human relationships, as the lure, aim, and agency for effecting love
in the world, Jesus manifested that God is change itself. God is both the supreme and enduring loving one
and also related to, actively involved in, and affected
by all that goes on in creation.

As applied to the individual Catholic, the strategy means taking on a new awareness, the recognition
that humans are continually changing and developing.
Indeed, it means the realization that those moments
of clash and uncertainty which occur at the awkward
junctures and transition points of life are the periods
of ultimate creativity. Humans have a special history
and a promising and remarkable future if they carry out
their responsibilities for actualizing love in the
world during their process of growth. The critical
threshold which emerged through Jesus pushed forward
the unfolding drama of evolution for all humanity and
from that point on, all persons are called to carry
on evolution and bring the world closer to completion
through their dynamic efforts of love and service to
others. Conscious of their freedom and mission to
express personal initiative, Catholics are challenged
to move from safety and security, to seek those new
ventures which may become potential revelations of the
Spirit.

The solution or goal is an awareness and realization of the Kingdom as the reign of absolute love in
the world, centered on the risen Christ who is both
the personal center of the entire world and the point
of its final consummation -- its "Omega Point." The
goal is a sharing in the resurrection of Jesus as the
sign of victory, the symbol of the triumphant love of
God at work in the world and in human life. It is the
vision of a new humanity, a commonwealth of persons
united in selfless love. The divinity of each person
is recognized. This is nothing less than a "cosmo-
genesis," the creation of a new heaven and a new earth,
a world where there is the emergence of the mystical

Body of Christ and a Christ-consciousness in each
person. It is a new world where the love of Jesus
is embodied in life and action and conveyed to others
until eventually all of humanity is included. When
that moment comes, the process will be completed and
God will be all in all.

Story

A fourth option is the theology of "story."
John Dunne and John Shea are two of the many theologians who use stories and myths to open our sensibili-
ties to some of the hidden or lost dimensions in ourselves that have to be discovered before we can become
whole persons. This theology presumes that myths are
stories that contain the fundamental religious truths
of a culture, describing exemplary and universal
action and calling for imitation of the gods they describe and total participation in the adventures of the
heroes they recount. Myths are studied not so much
for what they mean as for what they can tell us about
our own meaning. Myths provide a way of living with
tragic, threatening, and intolerable situations, not
by explaining them away, but by relating them to
divine activity. Biblical stories, for example, are
considered as stories of invitation and decision, a
presentation of a cosmic picture where human history
is just one theater of the action of the combat between
good and evil. The invitation comes not from a metaphysical God, but a God-in-action, incarnate in Jesus
Christ. The decision is made by each person whose life
is a quest for psychological wholeness or a journey
toward spiritual wholeness. Myths and stories, open
to many frames of reference and different levels of
meaning, help explore the possibilities of that quest
and journey.

The problem from this theological perspective is
more individual than in any of the earlier options.
The social dimension, though it is an essential component in psychological development, tends to be only
a secondary factor. The problem is this: How can I
make sense out of life, how can I find a direction
which can serve as the basis for my future actions and

judgments? How can I determine who I am in the light of my individual experiences, convictions, and interpretations? How can I give a structure and a thrust to my experiences in a way that does not limit them but enables them to contribute to my sense of personal fulfillment and personal responsibility in and for history?

The strategy consists in following Jesus as the hero of the quest stories. His journey was an exodus to the Father, a pilgrimage. Like the heroes of other religious cultures, Jesus went on a journey of separation and return, descent and ascent. In the separation He did not cling to His divinity but emptied Himself and underwent a series of trials and temptations from the dark forces of evil. While He was uprooted, He gradually came to a consciousness of who He was and what His mission was. Engaged in battle with those powers of evil that threaten all human life and meaning, He even took on the humiliating status of a slave. Only after the struggle could He return to His Father in glory. His separation from security occurred often in His life. In fact, it occurred each time He experienced a major turning point in His life, for example, at His baptism, at the beginning of His preaching, and at the awareness of His death. Each time Jesus was faced with an awesome decision He grew in human consciousness and gradually discovered His true self, which was both human and divine.

The strategy for Catholics following this option is to recognize that the hero patterns in the stories of Jesus provide a precious structure of meaning into which they can fit the moments of their personal existence. By passing over and participating in the standpoint of Jesus, they will gradually realize what God is doing in their lives. Enthused by an awareness of their unconditional acceptance by God, they will recognize that God brings humanity gifts of peace, sustenance, wholeness, and life that no rational scheme can explain. To acknowledge that life is a journey with critical points of passage demands strenuous effort, yet the gifts that God brings makes that effort worthwhile. By regarding the story of

Jesus as a quest and search for His own personal identity and by making that story their own, Catholics have an exemplary model to follow. By sharing the journey of Christ, they can reflect on the odyssey of their own spirit and explore the wilderness of their own selfhood. They can become conscious of themselves as unique individuals, and by responsibly confronting the unknown and contradictory forces within themselves, they gradually make their way to the homecoming with their common Father.

The solution or goal is the homecoming, or return, of the hero, through His death and resurrection, no matter how intense the struggle. Symbolically this homecoming is an image of the building up of the Kingdom of God through a greater awareness of each person's sharing in the image of God. The homecoming is the rebirth of human consciousness that comes when persons come into touch with their true identity as both human and divine. The homecoming is the successful completion of a paschal journey to the Father, that is, a passage from suffering to glory, culminating in a victory celebration. The homecoming is the conclusion of a pilgrimage where God is encountered not only at the end, but in the struggles along the way. It is the recognition that life, with its crises of adolescence, its mid-life transformations, and its gift of wisdom in due time, is an adventure with unexpected risks rather than a safely planned journey. What supports the adventure is the recognition that God is present as the source and support in the midst of these struggles. Life then has meaning because persons see themselves as acting jointly with God even while they are on the way to the Kingdom.

Encounter with World Religions

The fifth, and final, example of current theological faith options overlaps with some elements of the others. This last option, a "theology of encounter with world religions," is representative of the thinking of persons as diverse as Thomas Merton and Raimondo Panikkar. It draws its vitality from a turn to Eastern religions and their emphasis on mystical experience and the depths of the self. It attempts to relate the contemplative life to the world of political involvement in which Catholicism's historical destiny is played out. Drawing insights from Hinduism, Taoism, and Buddhism, for example, this theology expands and enriches the perspectives from which to view God, human nature, and the universe. It opens dimensions which heretofore have been either closed or unnoticed. The very foreignness of these Eastern religions makes them appear more real, vital, and usable.

The _problem_ as perceived from this last perspective will vary with each religion encountered. In general terms the problem might be described as a contagion of one's own obsessions and egocentered ambitions, or as a delusion about ends and means due to one's own doctrinaire prejudices. More specifically, the problem may be human ignorance, social chaos, the suffering in the world caused by immoderate desire, or the illusion that the world of appearances is real. In other words, human life is a life of alienation oscillating between hope and despair as a result of ignorance and overdependence on the individual self. The search for truth is all the more elusive as people are mesmerized by a world that is becoming more and more technological and institutionalized.

The _strategy_ consists in seeing the uniqueness of the insight and experience of Jesus. The founders of various world religions each had a particular perspective on reality that generated a religion. For example, social chaos can be overcome by social order, suffering can be vanquished by destroying selfish desire, or right action consists in acting without seeking the fruits of action. Jesus' unique insight was His awareness of God as a loving Father who calls all persons to share His divine life. This was His Gospel, His Good News, for all humanity. Jesus' resurrection was the stamp of divine approval on His earthly life and ministry. This unique insight and resurrection experience provides all Catholics with an answer to the ultimate questions of life, suffering, and death. Jesus, through His unique insight and experience, becomes the center of religious experiences for His followers, the renewing agent, the ultimately

decisive and definitive exemplar for their relationships with God and other persons.

As applied to individual Catholics, this <u>strategy</u>
becomes effective if they meditate on the insights of
those religious figures who have made the journey of
inter-religious experience an integral element in
their interpretation of their own faith-tradition.
Such meditation may be the source of strength for
their own religious experience. Empathy toward other
faiths, far from diminishing confidence in one's own
tradition, can be the source of a deepened understanding of that tradition. In studying the modern Hindu
Gandhi, for example, Catholics can acknowledge the
necessity for inner change that brings self-transcend-
ence as the only possible means for peace on earth.
From Taoism Catholics can learn to truly listen in
silence and solitude with a heart that is at peace,
detached, and without care. They can learn to acknowledge the Biblical Word as a divine gift, demanding a
response that recognizes the world as in a state of
flux between opposites, between Yes and No; a world
in which what seems right from one point of view may
be completely wrong when seen from a different aspect.
From Buddhist compassion, they can learn something
about love; from Buddhist enlightenment, they can learn
about conversion; from Buddhist Nirvana, they can learn
a mode of perceiving and being in the world, a way of
dwelling in fuller awareness in the present moment, a
way of bestowing devoted attention on even the smallest
particulars of daily existence. From the Eastern
religions in general, they can find a different perspective on the relationship between contemplation and
action. Integrity and full personal development come
through engaging the world at a deeper level, not
necessarily through political deeds, but through culti-
vating and acting upon a consciousness and awareness
of the positive nature of love in healing the sickness
of crimes, war, and political tyranny.

The goal or <u>solution</u> in this final theological
option is the Kingdom of God, seen as the sharing of
a new awareness, a recognition of the reality of the
divine will for the salvation of all humanity. It
is a share in the resurrection of Jesus, seen as the

taking on of a new life of perfect integration, complete fulfillment, and total liberty of spirit. From this perspective the Kingdom of God and the Resurrection are present realities, manifested in the Catholic Church which is the sacrament or symbol of the salvation that is gradually being realized in the world. The goal is a certain maturity of consciousness, where Catholics see themselves as moved by the grace of God and are able to dispel all kinds of pettiness with regard to their own religious tradition and all prejudices regarding other traditions. From the Eastern perspective, the goal or Kingdom is a certain "nothingness," a self-emptying, where the light and glory of God are manifested in their full radiation, as the individual recognizes the human self and the divine self as a single entity.

Conclusion

In this chapter we have looked at some of the rich variety of faith options open to Catholics. Before we could do this, however, we had to distinguish between belief as doctrine and belief as faith. The relatively few doctrines of the Catholic Church, which have at their core the Incarnation and Resurrection of the God-man Jesus, do not change over the centuries. The interpretation and faith responses to these doctrines do change, however, with each generation.

After reviewing the classical theology of redemption, we looked at four of the many modern theological options which may help Catholics both to understand and to express their faith in a meaningful way. All four of them (liberation, process, story, and encounter with world religions) are deeply rooted in the Christian heritage and attempt to make it relevant today. No option is the only way nor is any one independent from the others. Each is a paradigm of faith which, when lived, overlaps with the others. Indeed, many theologians could be identified as representatives of several of the options we presented. The options all attempt to involve Catholics in committing themselves to arriving at the Kingdom through the strategy of responding to God's call by following and imitating

Jesus the God-man.

Each option gives a slightly different insight into the Catholic heritage. Some are more personal and internal in orientation; others more social and external. Some lead to contemplation rather than action; others lead from involvement in the world to meditation. Some highlight the necessity of changing perspectives throughout life; others stress an unchanging focus or vision. One is an inner pilgrimage; another is a geographical one. One sees alienation as a problem of society; another sees it as a problem of the self. Some stress the present; others the future. All of them are attempts to make valid and personally meaningful the basic insights found in the Catholic heritage, whether in the Gospel proclamations or in the more philosophical doctrinal formulations through the centuries. All of them, to be effective, demand a respond to God's call to share in His divine life and to help create the Kingdom which He wishes to share with all humanity.

QUESTIONS

Personal Reflection

1. Do you believe? In what? In whom? Mention at least two beliefs.

2. Who is the best example of believing you know? Why?

3. Whom do you trust the most?

4. Is Jesus real to you?

5. Of the five options of faith we discussed which makes the most sense to you? Which do you think is the best? Why?

Group Discussion

1. What is the biggest problem in the world, which, if solved, would make all of us happier?

2. Is it possible to trust anyone completely?

3. Get a copy of the creed you say on Sunday. How much of it can you explain? Is there any statement you have difficulty believing? Does logic have a place in matters of faith?

4. What does it mean to have faith in Jesus? Do you know anyone who does?

5. Rank the various faith options starting with the one you think most people believe.

Review Questions

1. State, with examples, the meaning of belief, doctrine, and faith.

2. Why are doctrines necessary?

3. What is the relationship between faith and doctrine?

4. What does a theologian do?

5. State and explain the five options of faith.

SUGGESTED READINGS

Dunne, John
Time and Myth
University of Notre Dame Press, 1978

An analysis of humanity's inevitable confrontation with death and various attempts to resolve it through stories of God and ordinary people.

Haughton, Rosemary
The Catholic Thing
Templegate, 1980

A wide-ranging look through Christian history, literature, and biography to provide a description of that Catholicism which is larger than the institution.

Hellwig, Monica
Tradition: The Catholic
Story Today
Pflaum, 1974

A contemporary appraisal
of the Catholic heritage,
its history of hope and
heroes, its folklore and
fantasy, its community
traditions.

McBrien, Richard
Who is a Catholic?
Dimension Books, 1971

A succinct and cogent
survey of the meaning of
Catholic life and its
urgent challenges today.

Merton, Thomas
Mystics and Zen Masters
Dell, 1969

A study of the ways of
meditation and spiritual
experience in both Eastern
and Western religions.

Migliore, Daniel
Called to Freedom
Westminster Press, 1980

A restating and rethinking
of five basic Christian
doctrines in the light of
liberation theology.

O'Collins, Gerald
The Case against Dogma
Paulist Press, 1975

A new perspective, both
historical and epistemolo-
gical, on the whole idea
of dogma, showing that it
has outlived its useful-
ness as a theological
category.

Shea, John
Stories of God
Thomas More, 1978

Use of story theology and
myth to make the Biblical
Good News come alive for
a new generation.

Sobrino, Jon
Christology at the
Crossroads
Orbis, 1978

A study of Christology
from the perspective of
the liberation theology
of the Third World.

IV. OPTIONS IN CHRISTIAN LIVING

DANIEL BROWN

On August 9, 1943, Fränz Jägerstätter, a young Austrian peasant, died at the executioner's block in a Berlin prison because he refused induction into the army on the grounds that it was contrary to his belief as a Christian. Although court officials assured him that he could serve in a non-combat role such as medical corpsman or clerk if he accepted induction and his wife and family pleaded with him, Jägerstätter would not change his mind. He likewise refused the advice of his parish priest, prison chaplains, bishop, neighbors, and friends. These people spoke movingly of Jägerstätter's obligations toward his family, the hardships his stance would bring them, and the pointlessness of his resistance. His resistance until death would make no difference, they said. The war would go on. Hinting that pride prompted his resistance, they asked him to consider the harm he was doing to others. Everything these friends predicted came to pass. Jägerstätter was executed. His wife and three small daughters suffered because of it. The war in Europe continued for almost two more years.

Questions

In reflecting on this story, one can ponder many things about it and about the man. Was Jäggerstätter a well-meaning but misguided soul? Was he a fanatic? Was he a menace who did not understand the meaning of human life for his wife and family? Was he temporarily or permanently mad? Or was he a thoughtful person who weighed the consequences of his convictions?

People who knew him and those who have studied his life and writings judge him as a simple, careful, unaffected, pious person who loved his family and did not want to die. Further, it appears, he did not consider his actions heroic or normative for others.

He felt his position stemmed from God's grace to him alone.

This story raises other questions that are not limited to a judgment about this man and his time but are more universal in scope. Who is the good Christian? Are these good people to be imitated? What demands does a person's vocation as a Christian make upon the individual? Does the conscientious Christian imitate the lives of holy predecessors? What is holiness today?

In answering these questions, I want to point out that I feel the questions are better than the answers and that the questions will still remain even after I have answered them. Further, I expect that you may answer these questions differently from the way I do; surely you will answer them differently 15 years from now.

The Good Person

Who is the good person? Throughout history people have been judged to be good because they were heroes, doers of kind deeds, clowns, clever and talented, or lovers. Philosophers and other sages have discussed the good person and the term "goodness" in abstract and concrete terms. Playwrights, poets, storytellers, and novelists have fashioned characters they consider good, although often they are less engaging or memorable than their villainous counterparts.

"Good persons act in a generous way for themselves and others. They act in a just way and enable others to do the same." I like this description of the good person because it suggests action in contrast to complete passivity. Undesirable events lead the good persons to act one way when they may have wanted to do something else, but, however unwillingly, they do not remain inert. This description pictures the good person as acting on behalf of self or society. Sometimes the self and others can benefit simultaneously, but often there is a tension between them. The good person's actions may lead to conflict and even suffering, but they do not set out to hamper the rights of others, to inflict pain, or to seek advantage at the expense of others. Finally, this description points to the power of the good person to empower others to be good. This empowering may take the form of inspiration and imitation as well as the legal and physical connotations of power. The New Testament story of the prodigal son and the forgiving father who takes him back into his house illustrates the empowering we speak of. The forgiven son could presumably act the same way as his father once he was restored to the family circle. That would be quite laudable, but the father's action empowers the son to do even more than imitate a generous, forgiving gesture; they, in fact, open up a new life for the son. It should be pointed out that empowering others to be good is not equated with success. Socrates would be an example of a good person whose success in this life was modest at best, but who enabled others to be good by his teaching, his methods, his life, and his death. Franz Jägerstätter likewise met little success in his lifetime. Whether he enables others to be good after his death remains an open question.

The Good Christian

Who is the good Christian? The term frequently employed to describe good Christians is the word holy, and many people in the history of the Church have been described as such, Augustine of Hippo, Thomas More, Teresa of Avila, and Franz Jägerstätter to mention a few. Each of these was a very different person, so one might ask why they are called holy.

The second chapter discusses revelation and the significance of Jesus. That discussion, combined with what has just been said about a good person, leads to a description of what a good Christian is: The good Christian is fully committed to act with generosity and justice, and enables others to become more fully human because of the revelation of God.

For the Christian, God's revelation discloses that

the mystery of human life is more than a biological given, but a project filled with meaning and hope. Jesus' life, death, and resurrection hold a unique place in Christian history. Jesus reveals this mystery as no one else can. He empowers others to participate in the fundamental hopefulness of life. By Jesus' conquering the powers and principalities of the world, He has effectively overcome the idolatry of accepting anything less than God as worthy of ultimate allegiance. Jesus is the first member of a new people, a people we are called and empowered to join.

The earliest Christians were often called disciples of the Lord or followers of the way. "When he (Paul) got to Jerusalem he tried to join the disciples but they were all afraid of him; they could not believe he was really a disciple." (Acts 9:26) "When Priscilla and Aquilla heard him (Appollos) speak they took an interest in him and gave him further instruction about the way." (Acts 18: 26) The images connected with these terms -- disciples and followers of the way -- have remained. Christians have seen themselves as disciples or students, always eager to learn something new from the master or from their fellow disciples. The education of the Christian never ends. In a similar way, Christians see themselves on a road making a journey through life. As pilgrims they have no permanent resting place, only provisional ones along the way. The way often proves dangerous or lonely, but the travelers have confidence that their journey is not in vain.

It is now time to return to the people whose names we mentioned before, people who were in their own way disciples and travelers of the way, that is, good Christians.

Augustine (354-430 A.D.) lived in North Africa. His life and conversion show that he had a sensitive mind and that he changed dramatically because he thought God wanted him to change. Augustine wrote and preached prolifically. His work is ponderous more often than not, but the reader is struck by his clever and engaging insight into human life. Few

94

people have ever taken this world as seriously as did Augustine. Few have come to grips with the relationship between their political and social life and their Christian commitment. Many people do not agree with Augustine, but the issues of politics, conversion, and grace that he confronted have engaged Christians in the same way he faced them. Because of his demanding reflections on human nature and human society, no thinking Christian made familiar with Augustine can address the world superficially again or take this world and its society for granted.

A layman and Chancellor of England, Thomas More (1478-1535) was a paragon of personal integrity and a warm, loving family man. He fell afoul of royal power because of an unwavering sense of right and wrong. He did what he could to escape danger by keeping silent about his disagreements with Henry VIII, but he was too prominent a figure and silence was not enough for Henry VIII. In his conscience, More simply could not submit to the king's wishes. Few Catholics today maintain the notion of the papacy that Thomas died for. But he held these religious beliefs. They came into conflict with his political allegiance, and for maintaining them he was put to death.

Teresa of Avila (1515-1582) was an indefatigable reformer of convent life. Reform is never popular among those being reformed, but in 16th century Spain it was also dangerous. What she is perhaps most remembered for is her insistence on the individual's immediate relationship with God. For fear of being charged with heresy, Catholics of her time were eyed with suspicion if they did not promote ecclesial piety. She insisted on an entirely different dimension of Christianity. Throughout her book, The Interior Castle, she portrays God as a bold knight rewarding the just and punishing the wicked after he has tested them. But in the last section of the book, God puts aside this battle attire and suckles the soul with breasts as a mother does a newborn. The intimacy and care of God is much closer for her than official prayers and theology of the time would permit.

Jägerstätter led an unexceptional life but underwent a gradual religious conversion. He became convinced that he could not cooperate with any group that
opposed the commands of the Gospel. He refused to
take part in the activities of the Nazi youth organizations and then refused military service. He could
have escaped the death penalty by accepting induction
and then being assigned to non-combat duty, but he
refused to compromise. He paid with his life.

Imitation

Are we to imitate these holy people? Are we to
take them as models and try to pattern our lives on
theirs? At one time there was a movement in Catholicism that urged everyone to judge a situation by
saying "what would Jesus have done in this case? Is
there something in His life that would give me a clue
about what I should do?" In effect this approach
advocated a slavish imitation of Christ.

It is clear today that following in some ethereal
footsteps of Christ is not the only way to be holy.
The Christian seeks to share the same will Christ had
to establish God's reign of justice and to share His
resistance to giving allegiance to anything less than
His Father's reign. Imitation of Christ refers to
imitating His attitudes rather than specific actions.
To imitate Christ one does not have to die on the
cross. One does, however, have to seek to do God's
will. The two attitudes -- serving God's reign of
peace and justice and resisting total allegiance to
anything less than this -- can be imitated. One is not
required to imitate the exact way Jesus practiced these
attitudes. Thus the Christian resists the demands of
any institution, even one's nation, which pretends to
be supreme. In the 20th century, Nazi Germany comes
immediately to mind as a nation which demanded total
allegiance of its citizens. A Christian cannot give
total allegiance to any such demands.

Vocation and Career

What demands does a person's vocation as a

Christian make? In order to answer this question we first distinguish between career and vocation. A vocation literally means a _calling_. Christians believe that they are _called_ to establish God's reign of justice and to resist giving total allegiance to anything short of God's reign. Christians can, and do, give support to various institutions like one's country, one's business, one's sports team, but this support is limited by their deeper allegiance to God's reign.

A career is one's work. Any career which demands ultimate allegiance for something that gives ultimate fulfillment is idolatry. Holy people have revealed or testified to this with their lives. Careers have often interfered with vocation and vocation has also wrecked promising careers, as in the case of Thomas More. To distinguish between vocation and career is not to separate them, however. Frequently, in fact, they support one another.

The examined Christian life consists in seeing what demands this vocation makes on a person in the concrete situations of life. Is one's career at odds with one's vocation? How does one set career and vocation straight?

In the past there used to be two separate categories for the study of theology, one called moral theology and the other called spiritual theology. Moral theology usually considered what was right and what was wrong, what was permitted to the Christian and what was not. Basically, it was a rather negative thing, concerned especially with sin and how to avoid it. Spiritual theology, on the other hand, was much more positive. It dealt with sanctification: "How does the good person become better?" Today these theologies seem to be largely joined because we are not dealing with separate realities of the holy and sin, but one reality, the Christian life, the Christian vocation. One's career may support one's vocation, but it never replaces it. Being Pope does not lessen the vocational demand of supporting the establishment of God's reign.

Fundamental Option

Many Catholic theologians subscribe to a position that is termed a fundamental option. Briefly, it states that in life a person makes certain choices which are going to influence all the other facets of one's life. Because of that one choice or those few choices, others will follow upon them. If, for example, a high school student decides to become a doctor, that choice leads to several other choices and decisions. The student would have had to get good grades, go to college, again get good grades, take special courses in preparation for medical school, get into medical school and, again, get good grades. All of these other decisions were a part of the first decision to become a doctor. The advantage of this approach to dealing with Christian life is that it attempts to see things in perspective. If the student took an elective course or two in art or history, it would hardly obstruct the original choice to be a doctor. If, on the other hand, the student took only art courses, then getting into medical school would become impossible and would effectively alter the original choice, even though the student may protest that the goal was still the same. Individual actions usually do not constitute a departure from the fundamental option, nor do individual actions constitute arrival at the goal.

It is the same in Christian living. By choosing to be a Christian one automatically includes a whole series of other choices, but likewise excludes a series of other choices from consideration. One action or two is hardly going to disqualify anyone from being a Christian, but repeatedly acting contrary to that fundamental option would constitute a fundamentally different choice. In Christianity, that fundamental option is to be a Christian, to live according to the belief that God's reign is present and that we share in its establishment and unfolding. The possibilities of living according to this option are as varied as the careers one can choose.

Holiness Today

The life of the good person is probably indis-
tinguishable from the life of a good non-believer in
many ways. The main difference is that the holy person's actions also include his or her belief that God
has revealed in Christ that human life is fundamentally hopeful, that we act in accordance with that
hope even to the point of a cross, and that responsibility for life in not optional. Others may act as
good Christians do, but they don't necessarily share
our vocation.

How Have We Gotten Here

How have we gotten our models for Christian
living, our ways of life, our spiritualities?

The earliest disciples and followers of the way
were often martyrs and confessors who suffered for
the sake of their faith. During the first three centuries of the Church, other Christians esteemed them
and promoted them as women and men to be emulated. As
a result, martyrdom has always retained a place of
esteem in the Christian community.

The end of the persecutions eliminated the potential for martyrdom, so Christians looked around for
other heroic figures. The choice fell upon monks and
nuns whose lives were pictured as heroic in contrast
with the lives of their noble or common contemporaries.
Treatises in praise of the ascetical practices or
miraculous powers of solitary figures became widespread.
They became the functional equivalent of martyrs of an
earlier age, that is, they were heroes.

Many of these figures chose to live outside the
mainstream of their society. Some, especially those
living near deserts, vied with each other to perform
more spectacular feats. One group, known as the
stylites or column-sitters, took to living atop columns
for years at a time. One of their number, Daniel by
name, is said to have lived on his pillar for more
than 30 years, often haranguing the crowds that came

to see this phenomenon. Irish monks often became life-long pilgrims, moving from place to place and begging their sustenance in the name of Christ from the faithful, to the chagrin of the Church hierarchy. There are stories of these monks setting out to sea in open boats without oars, confident that the Lord would guide them safely.

These monks also introduced an element into Christian spirituality which has remained to this day, although it is most often found in religious communities: the spiritual director. These directors took charge of the spiritual life of the individual, encouraging and testing the person in every facet of life.

The early Middle Ages still favored the recluse or member of a religious order as the holy person, but during this time the notion of sanctity also became broader. Since everyone had an assigned role in medieval society, to be holy was to be faithful to that role. Each role had its own set of Christian virtues. Monarchs who were just and endowed churches were holy. Peasants who were pious and obedient were holy. Esteem followed careful, though not exceeding, observance of the role.

As society changed, so did some of the models of piety. In the 13th century, Francis of Assisi typified these changes. He broke with his family by leaving his mother and father. He broke with his society by following a strange occupation. He broke with the accepted form of religious life, monasticism, by establishing a more flexible and mobile form of religious life.

With the emergence of individualism during the 14th, 15th, and 16th centuries, the focus of spirituality shifted to the individual's relationship to God, a relationship which transcended the ecclesial structures without ignoring them. Thomas à Kempis' The Imitation of Christ, after the Bible the most read book in Roman Catholicism, was both effect and cause of this type of spirituality. Such 15th century Rhenish mystics as Meister Eckhardt and Henri Suso and the 16th century Spanish mystics like Teresa of Avila and John of the Cross likewise treated spirituality in these terms. For the most part, this type of spirituality exalted the structured religious life as the model of sanctity. Other Christian vocations, such as marriage, business, and the professions, were seen as threats to sanctity.

Popular piety, like devotion to the Sacred Heart, dominated Roman Catholic spirituality from the 18th through the 20th centuries. This popular piety is still found in many families: pictures of the Sacred Heart and statues of the saints abound in them. These spiritualities, occasionally with sound theological foundation, appealed to the emotions and tended to be individualistic in approach.

From the 4th century until recently the model of Christian piety was, with few exceptions, the member of a religious order. The piety offered to the laity tended to be an adaptation of that offered to members of religious orders.

American Spirituality

In the United States the Roman Catholic experience of Christian living has proved to be different from that of Roman Catholics elsewhere. Initially American Christianity, like white American experience in general, was an outpost of European life, often trying to reproduce its transatlantic ancestor. Catholicism, however, soon found that many European models would not work here. Immigrants and their children often retained and sometimes modified Old World customs, so that American Catholics became more than just transplanted Europeans. A style of being both American and Catholic has set them apart from the Catholics in other parts of the world. Many contemporary Catholics in the United States have rejected a radical dichotomy between heaven and earth, between the natural and the supernatural. Rather than rejecting earthly concerns, American Catholics have shown that there is no true Christianity without strong concern for this world and those in it.

One of the European dimensions of Catholicism
which Americans have inherited is clerical domination.
Overwhelmingly, leadership of the American Church has
been in the hands of clerics. As a result, the
spirituality stressed throughout the American Catholic
education system has been filtered through a clerical
screen. The principal American authors on the spiritual life have been clerics. Institutes on spiritual
life and the academic study of the spiritual life have
almost all been the preserve of the clergy.

Lay leadership, however, has been strongest in
the realm of social justice. Enclaves of lay Catholics have taken positions of leadership inside and
outside the Church in trying to stand firmly in the
gospel tradition of proclaiming and sharing in the
establishment of God's reign of justice. Catholics
have been involved in most social justice movements
including labor unions, political reform groups,
consumer groups, the Knights of Labor, the American
Federation of Labor, and Common Cause.

The status of American Catholics gradually shifted from oppressed minority to comfortable middle
class. To be sure, black, brown, and red Catholics
are as oppressed as their non-Catholic brethren.
Roman Catholic women not only share the discrimination
visited on their non-Catholic sisters, but suffer the
added handicap of sex discrimination within the Church.
Socially and economically Roman Catholics are better
off than other Christians in America. They are
wealthier, more educated, and more powerful. How does
one preserve one's identity as a Catholic in this
relatively new position of power? What are the idols
against which one must struggle today?

The situation is fairly new and so the answers
are still being formulated. The inherited tradition
provides clues about attitudes, but the concrete
forms still have to be worked out. The attitudes of
establishing God's reign and resisting idolatry seem
clear enough. But it is also certain that Catholics
will be allied with many non-Catholics in the pursuit
of their vocation. It also seems certain that Catho-

lics will often have to react to an agenda of items in
personal and social life which they have not determined.
The technologies of this age often create issues that
people might have wished to avoid, such as nuclear
proliferation and some medical experimentation.   It
might have been easier to search for a peaceful settle-
ment to international disputes if only two nations
possessed nuclear weapons instead of the ever increasing number who possess them.   Likewise, it might have
been easier to deal with the allocation of scarce
medical resources if preventive environmental measures
had been employed rather than having to develop new
medical technologies to deal with radiation sickness.
Willingly or not, a responsible Christian spirituality
has to deal with these issues and integrate them into
the vocation of announcing God's reign.

Options

There was a time not too long ago when many
Catholics considered it necessary that Catholics have
a unique position on every topic in every discipline.
The autonomy of disciplines such as politics, economics, and the exact sciences is now beyond question.
Piety is no substitute for proficiency in any scholarly
field, whether that field is physics or philosophy,
traffic control or theology.   The vocation of Christians addresses ultimate questions, but their lives are
not made up of only ultimate questions.   Their careers,
for example, are almost always made up of intermediate,
penultimate, or even trivial questions.   Since we do
not live in a two-storied universe of the natural and
the supernatural, one meets the ultimate only piece-
meal, in less than ultimate questions.   By being profi-
cient in one's work, one can advance one's career, but
the career is not all of one's life.   There is also a
deeper dimension, namely the vocation, the ultimate
goal of a person's life.   The vocation dictates the
basic commitment to establishing God's reign of justice in society and in the self.

To be a clerk in a store, for example, may seem
quite unradical, but one's vocation can still be faith-
fully pursued through the integrity with which the work

is done and the care taken in dealing with people. But the career, clerking, does not exhaust the possibilities of the vocation.

A person's life more than words embodies his or her values. One can talk about justice but quite easily end up being racist by remaining silent in the face of unfair housing laws. One might proclaim a personal inclination for equality without even considering the inherent sexism of the structures one supports. Time and circumstances conditioned the holiness of Christians in the past. The popes occupying the chair of Peter in Thomas More's time were personally reprehensible as well as inept, but what More supported transcended the individual pope. Today it could be that one sees obedience to God's reign best served by staunchly opposing those in power rather than supporting their just claims as upholders of the Christian tradition. Who knows how harsh the judgments of Christians 400 years hence will be upon this generation of Christians for its silence and inaction as well as its speech and actions? Continuity in holiness demands creativity, not slavish imitation.

For Catholics marriage is a holy institution. It is also the most common vocational choice among adult Catholics. Many Catholics of an earlier age considered marriage little more than a stable institution to foster the preservation of the human race. Recently, though, emphasis has been placed on marriage as a relationship of intimacy, growth, and love. By its lasting fidelity, Catholic marriage provides an opportunity to demonstrate that love overcomes hate and hope overcomes despair. When people commit themselves to each other they do so without reservation "in good times and in bad, in sickness and in health." This pledge has never been easy but it insists that the couple's love is of more value than health or good times, sickness or bad times. Groups such as the Christian Family Movement and Marriage Encounter attempt to support married people by providing a forum for mutual growth and peer support.

Celibacy is the positive decision to live an

unmarried, chaste life. One practical result of such a decision is that it allows more time and energy for promoting and proclaiming the presence of God's reign. Through a long evolutionary process what was originally a private choice of some priests became the mandated norm for all priests of the Western rite. While the legislative regulation making celibacy mandatory for priests has been questioned, such a personal choice will probably always have a place of esteem within the Church. Besides priests, many others in the Church publically profess a life of voluntary celibacy as members of religious orders.

The social implications of celibacy are clear. Celibates would die out in their first generation unless a larger community were willing to support them by encouraging others to join their ranks. This support has been crucial for the psychological well-being of celibates. Mutual prayer and support groups among celibates have developed in America in the last decade in order to amplify such support.

Prayer

In a book dedicated to exploring the options for American Catholics there is not much room for categorical statements. Here, however, there is room. Here there is no option: one prays or one is not a Christian. Writers have distinguished various types of prayer forms and it is here that options lie. We shall mention a few of them.

Private prayer is as venerable in Catholic tradition as liturgical prayer, which will be discussed in the eighth chapter. Private prayer complements liturgical prayer. It underscores the immediate relationship of the individual with God. Reciting formulae taken from the scriptures such as the Our Father or the Hail Mary has been one favorite type of private prayer practice. Set prayers composed at other times have also served the same purpose. By constant repetition the individual commits them to memory and no longer has to be caught up with individual words but can get beyond them to their sense.

Another form of private prayer has been the medi-tative reading and reflection on the scriptures or some other spiritual writing. The Roman Catholic reader considers these texts life-giving.

Prayers have also been distinguished by their purpose, regardless of their form. Thus there are prayers of adoration, petition, thanksgiving, and pardon. One adores by recognizing one's limitedness and by trusting that God fills up this incompleteness. Petition is when the individual recognizes responsi-bility for acting sinfully against one's vocation and asks pardon of the Lord. Petition and thanksgiving are two sides of the same coin. We recognize that all of life is a gift and we are its beneficiaries whether we are in a posture of gratitude or of petition.

All sincere prayer and practice of prayer have some things in common. First, they attempt to formu-late in words, thought, or feelings God's will in our lives. By putting into words what one experiences, we constantly redefine our personality by examining our own life and God's will for us. Second, they are a reflection and extension of our entire life. They may focus attention more clearly on that life, but they are not a separate reality. Our prayer, if sin-cere, will reflect on life and our life will embody the words, thoughts, and feelings of the prayer. Pray-ing for peace will bespeak a life in pursuit of peace. Praying for forgiveness will indicate a life of for-giveness. Third, prayer is persevering. Emotion and a feeling of satisfaction may accompany prayer, but they may also be missing. When they are absent, how-ever, we do not stop praying. There is no good time for prayer just as there is no bad time for prayer. Like breathing, prayer may feel better at certain times, but people die if they breathe only when they feel good about it.

Recently, many Catholics have felt the need for a more active prayer life, one which goes beyond the liturgy. Prayer groups, large and small, meet this need. A list of prayer groups may be found in any local Catholic newspaper.

Summary

The Catholic Christian is called to be a holy person, leading a life of commitment to proclaim God's reign and to embody it. This vocation takes precedence over all other commitments.

Franz Jägerstätter dramatically embodied this commitment. The demands will not be so taxing for most Catholics, but the commitment is the same.

QUESTIONS

Personal Reflection

1. Who is someone you consider good? Do you know why?

2. Could you describe your fundamental option? Look at your life until now. What do you think has most determined what you did and said?

3. Who helps you be good? How do they help you?

4. What or who is your greatest aid in following your vocation?

5. Are there any choices you would make which might help you live a Christian life?

Group Discussion

1. Does the "commitment to serve God's reign" differ from fanaticism?

2. Does our society give more attention to good people than bad ones? To good action rather than bad? Why do you think society gives such attention?

3. If you were to pick an example of a "good or holy" Catholic, who would it be? Describe the person.

4. Do you believe people make conscious fundamental options?

5. When you think of being holy, do you ever think you need others to help you?

6. Are there any careers which seem to interfere with a person's vocation?

Review Questions

1. Distinguish career and vocation.

2. What is a fundamental option?

3. Explain: "The examined Christian life consists in seeing what demands vocation makes on the person in the concrete situations of life."

4. Explain: "Piety is no substitute for proficiency in any scholarly field, whether the field is physics or philosophy, traffic control or theology."

5. "Prayer, if sincere, will reflect life and life will embody the words, thoughts and feelings of the prayer." How?

SUGGESTED READINGS

Bouyer, Louis
Introduction to Spirituality
Desclee, 1961

A scholarly presentation that provides a solid orientation.

Cunningham, Lawrence S.
The Meaning of the Saints

A contemporary reappraisal of hagiography, a field that seemed to have gone into eclipse in the recent experience of Catholicism.

Fox, Matthew
On Becoming a Magical Mystical
Bear: Spiritually, American
Style
Paulist Press, 1976

A readable account of spirituality.

Haring, Bernard
The Law of Christ 3 volumes
Newman Press, 1961

Ponderous, but one of
the first books to
show the essential re-
lationship between
spiritual and moral
theology.

a Kempis, Thomas
Imitation of Christ
Doubleday, 1976

Classically important.

Merton, Thomas
New Seeds of Contemplation
New Directions, 1961

Just one of his many
worthwhile books.

Murray, John Courtney
We Hold These Truths
Sheed and Ward, 1961

See especially his
chapter "Is It
Basketweaving?"

Nouwen, Henri
Reaching Out: The Three
Movements of the Spiritual
Life
Doubleday, 1975

Simple, readable, and
worthwhile, this book
was written by a
therapist interested
in spiritual matters.

Teresa of Avila
The Interior Castle
Doubleday, 1972

Not always easy read-
ing, but very strong
and historically
important.

Thils, Gustave
Christian Holiness: A Precis
of Ascetical Theology
Lanoo Publishers, 1961

Traditional, dry, but
useful.

Zahn, Gordon
In Solitary Witness: The
Life and Death of Franz
Jägerstätter.
Beacon Press, 1968

A solid and sensitive
account of a pacifist
way of life.

V. OPTIONS IN RESPONSIBILITY

DANIEL BROWN

Catherine Morris is a woman in her mid-forties. She had been a tennis star at U.C.L.A. and then a public school teacher. She entered a convent and became principal of a fashionable suburban Catholic girls' school. She left the convent, married, and currently lives on skid row in Los Angeles, where she and a group of other people run a hospitality kitchen and clinic. In the spring of 1979, Catherine and several other women blocked the entrance to an exhibition hall displaying advanced technlogical weapons. Because of this, she was arrested and charged with disturbing the peace and trespassing.

***

Like the story of Franz Jägerstätter in the previous chapter, how does one go from being a thoroughly respectable member of the civic and religious community to being arrested by civic authorities and avoided by most religious authorities? More important for this chapter, why does one do it? Was she being responsible? What leads one to act out of a sense of responsibility? What options are open to the responsible person?

How did we get here? Actions and Intentions

For the first millenium Christians did not ask about responsibility. Instead, they asked whether what a person did was good or bad. Actions were deemed good or bad in light of the results that they produced. Why someone performed an action, the intention, was not considered. In the 12th century, Peter Abelard introduced a new notion into the quality of human activity, namely the intention of the person acting. Just as an action with good results is not particularly good if one is forced to do it, so responsibility for an action with undesirable consequences may

110

be less dependent on the intention of the actor. Deciding on the responsibility for human activity means, therefore, going beyond results to consider intentions. A responsible act was seen as both action and intention.

Manuals and Casuistry

In the past, Church officials also judged actions right or wrong on the basis of what the Church taught about a given action. Little attention was paid to the intention of the individual Christian. Decrees of church councils, local bishops, or the Pope usually expressed the Church's teaching about right and wrong actions. For the most part, church officials considered moral theology to be concerned with specific issues of right and wrong. In the case of Catherine Morris, for example, moral theologians might have discussed the legitimacy of her action in blocking the entrance to the arms exhibition but they would have had little to say about her decision to work on skid row. They might have considered that choice of lifestyle laudatory, but they would consider it a matter for spiritual theology, not moral theology.

There was diversity on some issues. Positions changed at different times and places. During much of the Middle Ages, for instance, the Church took a very strong position against lending money at interest. But this position gradually was abandoned with the rise of Capitalism.

Church teaching filtered down to the faithful through preaching, catechisms, and manuals designed to assist confessors in judging the rightness or wrongness of an action. These manuals had a great influence in determining the mentality of many Catholics. Intended to help the priest in hearing confessions, they had a narrow focus, specifically answering the question "how far can I go in some action before it is a sin?" Daniel Maguire, a professor of ethics at Marquette University, likens these manuals to mountain-climbing guides that are concerned only with the question, "how far can I lean back before falling off the mountain?" "How far to lean back" is an extremely important chapter in such guidebooks, one which could be left out only at great risk. But it is a list of "don'ts" and not a description of mountain climbing. It misses all of the positive, exhilarating dimensions of the sport. The same can be said regarding Christianity. A Christian ought to know what sin is and how to avoid it, but that is not the heart of Christianity and that is why the previous chapter and this chapter should be seen together. They deal with Christian life as a continuum. Both consider the vocation of the Christian to proclaim the presence of God's reign and to live according to that proclamation. They are a guide to Christian living which reflects sin and the exhilaration of living.

These confessors' manuals served as the principal textbooks for moral theology in Roman Catholic seminaries for centuries. Written by clerics, they expressed a conservative, male bias, although some showed a remarkable amount of enlightened compassion. They stressed issues of personal conduct and familiar virtues. When they treated social issues, they encouraged submission to the Church and obedience to the state. The burden of proof for justifying any nonconforming activity lay with the individual. They clearly stated that ultimate responsibility for judging right and wrong always lay in the individual's conscience. But they went on to insist that the conscience must be properly informed, and that meant it should agree with the Church's teachings and practices. If a conflict arose between conscience and authority, conscience should be followed, but these books made it clear that a conflict would be rare between the informed conscience and Church teaching.

The methodology in these books was called casuistry because it took individual cases (casus in Latin) and applied general principles to these cases. The method deliberately left room for differences of opinion and for development. In practice, the differences were few and the entire enterprise often degenerated into legalism. Formulating guidelines for interpreting the law requiring abstinence from meat, for example, became a complicated discussion on the ingredients in soups and gravies.

European Catholicism gave birth to these manuals
and method, which found a congenial home in American
Catholic seminaries and, therefore, in much of American Catholic life. American priests generally adhered
to the principles laid down in the manuals when dealing with penitents or giving advice.

New Looks in Moral Theology

Theology began to take a fresh look at much of
Catholic tradition and practice in this century, especially in the last thirty years. Renewals in the
study of scripture, systematic theology, and liturgy
all had their impact on moral theology. Catholics,
especially those in countries with sizeable non-Catholic populations, became familiar with the ethical work
of scholars of other faiths. Practices and prohibitions long taken for granted came in for closer scru-
tiny and re-evaluation. At times, re-examination
reinforced these positions. For example, the use of
extraordinary medical procedures to maintain the life
of an obviously moribund patient has continued to be
considered unnecessary. At other times, these practices and prohibitions were dropped, usually quietly,
as in the belief that an exercise of sexuality outside of marriage is seriously sinful without exception.

The careful study of scripture led scholars to
recognize that previous generations frequently assumed
too much and projected their own concerns into the
scriptures instead of letting the scriptures speak for
themselves. One such example came from the story of
Onan (Genesis 38: 4-10). Onan refused to have children
by his dead brother's wife because they would not have
been considered his own, but his brother's. Because
he failed in this obligation to perpetuate his brother's name, an obligation known as the levirate law, he
was struck dead. But in their eagerness to condemn
masturbation and birth control, moral theologians
saw this story as a clear condemnation of these acts,
even calling them Onanism. They did not even consider
the Levirate law.

Scripture scholars also demonstrated that there are actually very few injunctions of the New Testament to which moral theologians may appeal. Jesus preached very little regarding morality. He proclaimed God's reign, but only by implication did He say how one must act. Specific examples of His prohibitions are few and far between. But over time people began to take more seriously what Jesus and the prophets before Him had said about justice and the establishment of peace. And so people like Catherine Morris considered it more responsible to disrupt the sale of weapons than to obey trespassing ordinances or prepare schedules for suburban high schools.

The renewed study of the liturgy led theologians to stress that a splendid ritual was empty if unaccompanied by a life which embodied the message of the liturgy. Coming together in the name of the Lord and proclaiming God's reign in ritual is an empty gesture unless the participants live the truths of that communion. One can glimpse the loveliness of God's reign in the liturgy, which shows that people can sit down at one table as brother and sister and share a simple meal knowing that this is more important than anything that may divide them. But this glimpse is not enough. The hungry are not fed at the liturgy, the sick and imprisoned are not visited, peace and justice are not achieved there. All of these things must be effected outside the liturgy. Conduct outside of church has to correspond with what is celebrated in ritual within church. Otherwise, worship becomes a sham.

Doctrinal theology, too, caused a revolution in the field of moral theology. Theologians began to say that any statement made about God has a corresponding statement about human beings. Thus, if God is called Father, all of humanity is brother and sister without exception. If God is called creator, then the world, His creation, needs tending. Responsibility for the life of this planet has been put into our hands. The world has not yet been finished, and thus we continue God's act of creation by our own action in the world.

Options

Moral theology, which describes the "ought" of human life, relies heavily on those other branches of theology which describe the "is" of life. This section discusses some of the ways that moralists go about their business and some of the issues that occupy them. There are six basic approaches to discovering how one ought to act responsibly. We shall consider each of them in turn.

Principles

The theory of judging action by principles is fairly clear. One holds values that are quite dear, such as the sacredness of life or the trustworthiness of human friendship. One then reduces these values to principles intended to direct one's actions. The principles are usually stated in a negative way, such as "do not kill" or "do not tell lies." The principle sets out the value. The work of the moralist is to apply the principle to the individual case. The principles usually come from some authoritative source, such as the scriptures, church traditions, or reason. These principles are applied fairly rigorously to stress the need for clear guidelines in human activity. The basic assumption in judging by principles is that human life is sufficiently homogeneous that universal rules can be constructed to meet all eventualities.

While she may not be a Catholic moralist, the Duchess of Alice in Wonderland comes close to this position. "You're thinking about something, my dear, and that makes you forget to talk. I can't tell you just now what the moral of that is, but I shall remember in a bit." "Perhaps it hasn't one," Alice ventured to remark. "Tut, tut, child," said the Duchess. "Everything's got a moral, if only you can find it."

Situation Ethics

Often seen in contrast to the method of operating by principle is that method called contextual or situation ethics. Proponents of this method react strongly

to the legalism of the previous method and point to
the utter uniqueness of every human action. There is
no principle that can cover each human action, and so
each person must decide individually at the time of
the action whether it is right or wrong. Proponents
of this method point out that what may be right to one
may be wrong to another or that what might be wrong
at one time may be demanded at another. Think, for
example, of medical procedures to combat pneumonia.
If the victim were eighty years old and also suffering
from terminal cancer, the chances are that urgency
would not be considered as great as if the victim were
half that age and not similarly afflicted with cancer.
The situation, these authors would maintain, is different in each case and, therefore, a different response
is called for. In the case of the otherwise-healthy
younger person, there is a much greater responsibility
to treat the pneumonia than there is for the older,
cancer-ridden patient.

Creative Morality

It seems that both of the previous methods,
morality by principle and morality judged by individual situations, are too sharply drawn. Most moralists,
therefore, strive to maintain the insights of both
methods. Values do get enshrined in principles intended to be guidelines for conduct, but circumstances
modify individual actions so that the principles may
not be applicable. By carefully examining each situation to determine just what is in fact at stake, who
is involved, and what the intentions are, one can
begin to determine what is right or wrong in a given
situation.

Science is involved in the enterprise of judging
human conduct, but art is also involved because the
moralist tries to seek creative solutions to an issue,
not just traditional solutions. Thus, an alternative
may seem eminently justified in a situation, but the
situation itself may be the result of an underlying
injustice that needs correction. Breaking a law to
overturn some particular wrong may be thoroughly justified, but correcting the underlying cause of the

problem may be an even more creative way of acting.
A few examples might help.

There are many older people who commit suicide in
nursing homes. Seeing the appalling conditions in
which many of them live and the isolation from their
families and friends may lead one to conclude that,
indeed, there was nothing morally reprehensible about
their taking their lives. But upon examination one
can see that more creativity is called for. One
should look at the conditions which led to their action, see them as unjust, and then rectify them.
Improving the nursing home or seeking an alternative
to it is a creative alternative to despair.

Consider a demonstrator who opposes some action
and pays the price by going to jail. But then consider the person who does not choose that method of
rectifying the situation but actively lobbies for a
change through legislation. Both actions may be quite
laudable, but which one is more creative? This author
certainly does not know. What is clear is that each
of these actions is more creative than just complain-
ing.

Kingdom Morality

In the previous chapter we have referred to the
theory of the fundamental option, the choice of following "the Way" in the manner of the early Christians.
This method of approaching the rightness or wrongness
of actions rarely sees individual actions as embodying
the full impact of one's fundamental choice. For instance, missing Mass on a holy day of obligation could
hardly be considered an action which means a person is
leaving the Roman Catholic community unless that person
clearly invest the action with this meaning. Similarly, performing a good action, such as helping someone
in need, does not mean that one exhausts the reality
of Roman Catholicism and thus get out of all future
responsibility for good acts. Following this methodology means judging actions in the light of one's
commitment to proclaim God's reign. Individual actions
fit into a much more integrated picture of a person's

life. Franz Jägerstätter's opposition to Nazism and Catherine Morris' opposition to arms exhibitions are not just remote acts. Rather, they are related to all other facets of these people's lives.

Personalism

Personalism is an umbrella term that has caused as many problems as it has illuminated. In an effort to overcome the sterility of an ethic that relies solely upon an external code of conduct, the proponents of personalism view all of Christian life as an unfolding dialogue of the individual with God, other people, and the world. All activity is seen as directed toward building up a personalist universe. People are used to the notion of promoting individual and inter-personal growth. But personalism insists that society and all of its institutions will be judged good or bad on the basis of their encouragement of the person. Efficiency can never subvert the needs of the person, nor can utility ever be the basis of worth. Thus the personalist says that the cripple is equally worthy of care as the productive member of society. The worth is intrinsic to the person and has nothing to do with how much the person can produce.

In many ways personalism is more of a principle than a method and the adherents of all moral methods have benefited by listening to the writers connected with it.

Conspiracy

Conspiracy has an ominous sound to it, but then many people think that all framers of ethical or moral theory are slightly sinister anyway. But the word has a simple etymology and a more positive meaning. The etymology refers to breathing together and the meaning refers to agreement.

In a pluralist society where no one religious or ethical tradition dominates, anything approaching public consensus has to come from a willingness to bracket differences and to agree, at least provision-

ally, on a common method of dealing with issues of
common concern. The wellsprings of moral conduct
in this country have generally been considered to be
Jewish, Catholic, Protestant, and secular-humanist traditions. In the conspiracy method, all partners agree
that a rational approach can be shared regardless of
differences of faith and that all partners are equal
in this discussion. Roman Catholics have often incor-
porated this thinking into their own positions by
calling it natural law, even though the term has been
repugnant to other members of the conspiracy because
of the different conclusions reached on some issues.
The provisional character of the conspiracy approach
recognizes that an ultimate statement of the "ought"
in human life will elude mortals, but that a lot of
less-than-ultimate statements can be made and can be
helpful, even though they need constant revision. An
example of this would be the halting efforts at enact-
ing civil rights legislation in this country. It was
clear early on in the civil rights movement that
lunchroom counters and public buses should not be
segregated on the basis of race. However, it took a
bit longer for many to see that the right to vote
should not be restricted on the basis of color either.
Than it became clear that equal pay should be given
for equal work whether the person is black or white,
male or female.

Issues

It is pretentious as well as impossible to try
to treat all moral issues in a few short pages, but
we shall deal with some of these issues in the hope
of stimulating further discussion of the available
options. For the sake of convenience these issues
have been called personal, interpersonal, and societal.
There is, however, a great amount of overlap. Any
newspaper, any day, will give a wealth of material for
discussion of these issues. They are as broad as life.

Personal

If the readers were asked to make a list of
things that they had a right to, what would be on that

list? These rights do not derive their legitimacy from one's family, country, or church, they come simply from the fact that a person is a person. Such a list would probably speak of a right to life, and therefore of a right to adequate nourishment and health. There would probably be something about the freedom to choose what we want to do with our lives as far as developing our own talents, and something about a right to education and work. Then there would probably be the right to choose a spouse or friends and the time to enjoy them. Further, there would be something about being able to express self without fear of reprisal.

If all of this sound like the Declaration of Independence and the Bill of Rights, it is no accident. Defense of life, liberty, and the pursuit of happiness have a long tradition that can be found in Christianity long before 1776 or 1789. Dealing with these rights, how far they go, and what to do when they conflict with the rights of others is the whole business of personal morality.

The sad fact is that long before and long after 1776 rights have been more often ignored than observed. Personal morality tries to insure their observance by providing a forum for discussing their implications.

Interpersonal

Interpersonal issues, clearly linked with personal and societal ones, likewise struggle to find enclaves where they might be treated carefully.

While sex is determined to conception, sexual stereotyping has often overwhelmed individuals by demanding certain types of conduct and excluding others. The ability to choose one's method of self-expression seems important, but since sexuality involves others, the rights of others can be safeguarded only if sexuality is carried on without exploitation. In the past, marriage was understood as the one place where sexual exploitation was prevented. Yet today it is increasingly clear that sexual exploitation may take place within, as well as outside, of marriage. In sex, as in everything else human, self-deception and mutual deception happen easily. Roman Catholics have clearly opted to support the exercise of sexual love within marriage as being less exploitative and more conducive to growth than sex outside of marriage.

Stereotypes have likewise victimized family life. The ideal family does not exist, and the real family is usually anything but ideal. Human beings all have deficiencies and these deficiencies become more apparent to those who live close at hand. Thus the family usually suffers more from a person's inadequacies than do any others the person is in contact with. Security, peace, and growth are burdens that are too heavy to expect a nuclear family to shoulder alone, even though it is in families that they seem to be best nurtured. Further, like the rights of the individual, the rights of the family to privacy are being threatened. Government interference is probably the least serious threat in this country when compared with economic pressures exerted from outside through peers and advertising to keep up with the neighbors.

Catholic tradition has considered divorce wrong, especially if followed by remarriage. Today, Catholics still view it as regrettable. Technically, it is still not admitted as a possibility for Catholics in Canon Law, although a much more liberal interpretation of the term annulment has recently amounted to something similar to divorce. In fact, however, many Catholics view divorce as a realistic response to an intolerable situation, no matter how regrettable the divorce may be. A marriage can foster love, encourage creative freedom, provide opportunities for growth, and stimulate generosity. But a marriage can also harm and prevent growth, as when the talents of one of the partners are squandered and resentment sets in. Divorce then could be a creative solution to stem the harm.

Society

Systematic ills admit of no simple solutions. Merely collecting like-minded people of good will does not provide a solution to societal problems. Individual

121

good will does not get handed over to the group. This can be seen in the following issues.

Take, for instance, racism and sexism. Helen Jaskoski, a professor of literature, including minority and women's literatures at California State University, Fullerton, has observed that all societies have been sexist and all have been racist. Centuries of practice make eradicating the evils overwhelming. Even becoming conscious of the examples of racism and sexism present in a society is a monumental task. Structured exclusion, even when not intended, frequently becomes so lodged and justified by seemingly responsible arguments that one can only hope for change with a passing of generations. The Church as well as other institutions is not exempt from the charge. Indeed, the Church has frequently lagged behind other groups by perpetuating racism and sexism.

Poverty, like so many other ills, has often been blamed on outside forces from bad weather to divine retribution. It is considerably more comfortable to deal with it that way because it shifts the burden of finding a solution somewhere else. But elimination of poverty is a matter of will on the part of those who possess the power to redistribute wealth. Where sufficient resources are present but there is vested interest in perpetuating the status quo, we have what has come to be called systematic sin, in other words, a changeable structure which is unjust. This is the world's situation today. Poverty goes beyond lacking adequate food to denial of access to education, health care, and culture. Unjust distribution of the earth's goods may not have been deliberately intended, but its perpetuation is culpable.

Catholics believe that the doctrine of creation can shed light on where responsibility lies. The doctrine affirms that the world is still being created. The task is now in the hands of people. Like God, we are also creators. Just as God brought order out of chaos, so we are to do the same. In this case the chaos is the victimization of the poor.

Militarism is another issue that requires examination. Closely aligned to poverty and frequently one of its causes is militarism. Aside from the incredible destruction that can be unleashed by nuclear, technological, total, or limited war, costly armaments enhance poverty by diverting resources away from basic needs to protection of wealth.

The way in which battles are fought has been of interest to Catholic moralists for a millenium and a half, ever since they realized that they did not have it in their power to stop wars. This way, they thought, they might at least be able to control some of the damage. Pacifism, the stance against all war and the advocacy of peace "in season and out of season," has become a more common minority position within Catholicism in the last twenty years. Selective-conscientious objection, the right to refuse participation in wars which individuals oppose for specific reasons, has been closely identified with Catholicism. There is, however, no provision for such a position in American law. Catholic moralists have also opposed nuclear war and "total" war, that is, the type of fighting which does not provide for the immunity of civilian populations.

The extent of militarism's power can be seen in America's conscription legislation. Citizens must prove that they are conscientiously opposed to military service in order to be excused from it. However, the persons inducted do not have to demonstrate that they are conscientiously committed to military service. There certainly have been conscientious soldiers who are convinced that only the proper use of force will be effective in combating an evil. Until such time as both warriors and objectors must prove their sincerity, the morality of any army is questionable. We cannot assume all warfare is moral.

Medicine is another controversial issue. Advances in technology have revolutionized the medical profession and have raised questions never posed before. Machines that can indefinitely prolong the breathing of otherwise-lifeless bodies raise questions about how such devices should be used and when a person can be considered dead. If resources are scarce, is there a justification for maintaining such life-support systems for the comatose? Should life-support systems be employed in order to keep organs fresh for potential donation? Who should have access to expensive dialysis machines? Only those who can pay? Or should people be chosen by lot? What rights do patients have who take part in medical experimentation? What obligations do doctors have in telling their patients about all the consequences of a medical procedure or a drug? What rights do the poor have to medical treatment? When should a doctor intervene surgically or medicinally with a pregnant woman? When is such intervention wrong?

All of these questions are new. And all require sophisticated answers because of the complex nature of the issues. Since their implications go far beyond the medical profession and touch the very quality of life itself, society must address them. Not to address these issues is to place the doctor both in the position of being the sole judge of right and wrong and in the position of making such decisions on an ad hoc basis.

Another issue of importance is business. To run a business usually means to make a profit. When little else is considered but the profit motive, trouble results and rights are usually transgressed. Business ethics is a broad field, covering the quality of work, the quality of working conditions, the honesty of presentation, marketing, and competition; and a concern for the environment. Businesses frequently claim that government controls or the concerns of consumer groups create a "negative business climate." They point, instead, to the benefits of business and industry. Without their contribution, they say, progress would be negligible at best and even greater poverty would result. Businesses have provided dangerous products and degrading working conditions, made false advertising claims, bribed others to obtain favorable markets or eliminate competition, and shown callous disregard to the environment, making their status as victim questionable. Likewise, labor has produced shoddy workmanship, resisted increased productivity and opposed mechanization in the name of protection, even though such actions ultimately hurt the consumer. All or any of these topics can provide sufficient material for a lifetime of ethical investigation inside or outside of business.

In a small business the accountable people are usually visible and can be held responsible. But in a large corporation, especially a multinational corporation, no such visible accountability is present. Sophistication is needed in business ethics to match the sophistication of business itself. The growth of business in the last fifty years renders obsolete earlier methods of judging business practices. To be outraged at some business practice may satisfy a need to register anger but does little to change the "is" of the wrong to the "ought" called for by morality. Outrage is an important but not sufficient expression of concern.

Does one, therefore, undertake extralegal or unconventional steps to stop the activity? Is sabotage justified as a corrective action? Should one protest continuing evil by demonstrating against it? Should one go to work for an unethical company with the intention of changing policy? Should one promote legislation to redress the current problem? Or, perhaps, should people shake the dust from their sandals and move elsewhere to create a less harmful society?

Summary

Christianity opposes the unexamined life. Responsibility for one's life, one's neighbor, and the world is part of the project of being human. Catherine Morris has taken responsibility by feeding hungry people, providing health care for the sick, poor, and opposing the use of scarce resources to improve the quality of weapons. Is there a more creative way of being responsible for this world?

QUESTIONS

Personal Reflection

1. What are five of your present responsibilities?

2. Are you worried about the consequences and responsibilities associated with your actions?

3. Of the six basic options of how to act responsibly, which are you most comfortable with in your daily life?

4. What medical decisions have had moral implications in your own life? How can you respond to them? Where would you go for guidance in making such a decision? Who would you talk to?

Group Discussion

1. Do you find the sacrament of reconciliation a judging of your right and wrong activities or an affirmation of your responsibilities? Do you find judgment a help in maturing? Do you find encouragement helpful in becoming a better person?

2. Can one live an unprincipled life and be a good Christian?

3. Of the six basic options, which do you think most people would associate with leading a good life?

4. Is divorce wrong? Is marriage wrong?

5. What responsibility does a manufacturer have to his or her customers beyond what is demanded by law? What responsibility do we have for our personal actions beyond those required by law?

Review Questions

1. What place does intention have in deciding whether an action is good or bad?

2. Is a moral theology based only on principles inadequate?

3. Is a moral theology based on the situation inadequate?

4. How can a fundamental-option approach to moral issues be deficient?

5. Does cooperation with others, in the conspiracy theory, effectively silence the Catholic voice in a moral issue by blending it with others?

SUGGESTED READINGS

Burtchell, J.
Philemon's Problem: The daily dilemma of the Christian
ACTA Publishers, 1973

A stimulating collection of essays on moral issues and other topics.

Duska, R. and Whelan, Mariella
Moral Development: a guide to Piaget and Kohlberg
Paulist Press, 1975

A good introduction to the way in which people develop a sense of right and wrong.

Cremillion, Joseph
The Gospel of Social Justice
Orbis Books, 1976

A sizeable collection of church statements on social issues from the recent past. An excellent introductory essay is included.

Johann, R.
Building the Human
Herder and Herder, 1970

A personalist philosopher deals with responsibility for the world.

Maguire, Daniel
The Moral Choice
Doubleday, 1978

One of the most readable and helpful introductions to morality and moral thinking around.

Martain, Jacques
True Humanism
Greenwood Press, 1970

One of the most famous 20th century Catholic thinkers addresses issues of the individual and society.

McCormack, Richard A.
"Notes on Moral Theology,"
Theological Studies.

For the past several years, Father McCormack has summarized the continuing discussion on all aspects of morality, both methodology and issues, in the leading journal of American Catholic theology.

Mounier, Emmanuel
Personalism
University of Notre Dame
Press, 1970

The principal spokesman for the Catholic philosophy of personalism in society.

Schnackenburg, Rudolf
The Moral Teaching of the
New Testament
Herder and Herder, 1965

Good, especially on what is and is not in the New Testament.

Shannon, Thomas, ed.
Biomedical Ethics
Paulist Press, 1976

A collection of essays on this enormous field.

VI. OPTIONS IN UNDERSTANDING THE CHURCH

ROBERT KRESS

The first question to come to mind when we hear
the word Church may very well be "why?" Why the
Church at all? This basic question has become even
more complicated today when there are so many different churches. Not only are there various Christian
churches. There are also Jewish, Muslim, Hindu, and
Buddhist churches, even though they may not use the
word "church" to describe themselves. Diversity such
as this is usually good. But these churches not only
differ from one another, they also seem to conflict
with one another.

So even if church in general were a good idea,
we would still be faced with a very difficult question.
Which of all these churches should one choose? Even
among the Christian churches with which we might be
more or less familiar there is a great variety. We
might consider some of them a bit odd. Some perenni-
ally predict the end of the world, some to the exact
date. When the day comes and the world does not end,
they go on as if they had never heard of such predictions. There are also the snake handlers in Appala-
chia, some of whom die each year because of the way
their church reads and interprets the Bible. When
they read "They will pick up snakes in their hands,
and be unharmed" (Mk 16:18), they pick up rattlesnakes
and copperheads. We might be tempted to write such
people off as crazy and go our way without another
thought about them, but we should really take them
into consideration. Not only do they belong to our
religious tradition, they also claim to be the Church
which Jesus Christ founded.

There are also groups called pseudo- or quasi-
religions. These groups live in a way that looks very
much like a traditional religion or church. They have
their own sacred books, hierarchy, ritual and liturgy,

conception of sin, Ultimate truth, idea of salvation, and they may excommunicate their errant members. They even have their own martyrs and may expect their members to become martyrs, if necessary. For instance, the formal apparatus of the official Communist party in countries such as Cuba, China and Russia manifests the equivalent of mostly everything that a traditional Church is. But such pseudo-religions and nontraditional churches also exist in Western democracies. It has become commonplace in academic circles to speak of the civil religion of the United States, since the nation itself acts in a way similar to a church or organized religion.

What has all this to do with the Catholic Church? And options within it? Very much, for it shows that there is a human need for what the traditional churches supply. When they do not fulfill this need, another organization will step in and fill it. Hence, the first option we have in regard to a church is not whether to belong to one or not. We shall do that in any case, in some way or other. The first option is really which church we will belong to. And this option brings with it a variety of other options. As we have seen, even within the single option of belonging to the Catholic Church there are many different options.

The fact that there are so many churches to join is a problem for Catholicism because it claims to be the special way, the Church. Vatican II still maintains that "this Church (of Christ) ...subsists in the Catholic Church which is governed by the successor of Peter and by the bishops"...(The Church, 8). The basis for this claim of specialness, but not identity, is found in the New Testament where Christians are said to constitute "the Way" (Acts 9:2). Jesus Himself said "I am the Way, the Truth and the Life" (Jn 14:6).

This Church, which subsists in the Catholic Church, is those people who accept Jesus as the Way and live according to this Way. Anyone who does not accept Jesus and the Church must automatically advocate some other way. They must have some other way of living, some other church. Does this mean that everyone has a

church? Yes. It is critically important that we understand that our primary option is not whether we
shall have a religion or belong to a church; the first
option is basically <u>which</u>, not <u>whether</u>.

The Church and Life

The Roman Church has always claimed, like Jesus
its source and founder, that it can say, "I have come
so that they may live and have it to the full" (Jn
10:10). We must judge the Church in the light of this
claim. Full life is certainly a wish that is rooted
deep in human nature. Mircea Eliade's historical
studies of world religions show that this desire for
higher and more life is found everywhere, among all
people. For example, his investigation about the
rites of initiation concludes that

> Initiation is equivalent to a basic change in
> existential condition; the novice emerges
> with a totally different being from that
> which he possessed before...he has become
> another. He returns to life a new man, assum-
> ing another mode of being. Its function must
> be understood in relation to what it prepares:
> birth to a higher mode of being...he is no
> longer a "natural man." (<u>Rites and Symbols</u>
> <u>of Initiation</u>, 1958).

One might be tempted to restrict such language and
strivings to the condition of early, primitive man.
In fact, many persons -- Feuerbach, Marx, Nietzsche
and Freud -- have claimed that such longing is just
make-believe, day dreaming, or wish fulfillment.

But despite such claims, we must ask ourselves
these questions. Is there anything beyond the everyday life we experience so immediately in our bodily
selves -- sometimes ecstasy, sometimes drudgery, but
always limited? Is there an object to our longing?
Is there anything beyond the limit of death? If so,
what is it?

The book of Wisdom in the Old Testament suggests
answers to these questions. It tells us that "Death

131

was not God's doing, he takes no pleasure in the extinction of the living. To be - for this he created all;" (Wisdom 1:13). St. Thomas always emphasized this text from Wisdom. He even went so far as to say that the power to take away one's existence does not reside in created things themselves. Only the Creator has such power. We emphasize here God's creative power not to cause an inferiority complex but to show how committed the Judeo-Christian tradition is to life and being. Such emphasis underlines the purpose of the Church as promoting life, not death. Jesus, who was not _of_ this world, was nevertheless very much _in_ it. He spent a goodly amount of His time healing the sick, raising the dead, consoling the grieved, in general, promoting life.

The option of being a Catholic means belonging to a group of people who think that the life-giving Jesus reveals a unique concept of the life-giving God and who organize their lives on this understanding.

Jesus: God With and For Us

Christmas songs and liturgy familiarize us with Jesus' title of Emmanuel or "God with us." We could also say that Jesus is "God's _for_ us." This is implied by Jesus Himself at the Last Supper when He gives us His body and blood in the Eucharist _for_ us. Jesus reveals that God is not against us, not far from us, but with us and for us. In its own way, the Church is and is supposed to act like God's "with" and "for" us. In the Christian religion, Jesus is the short-hand description for everything involved in salvation. That is what the Acts of the Apostles means when it says "For of all the names in the world given to men, this is the only one by which we can be saved" (4:12).

To be a Catholic means first of all to belong to that assembly of people who proclaim this Jesus-salvation. The Church is the Lord's Assembly. It is the Lord's in two ways: 1) The Lord called it together, so it belongs to Him; 2) It professes the Lord and dedicates itself to Him.

Describing the Church as the Lord's Assembly is important because it shows that the Church is not passive in regard to Jesus. Rather, God has created the Church in such a way that it can receive the Lord Jesus and thus be active in the accomplishment of the saving will of God, whose sole mediator Jesus is. The Church is that group of people who organize their lives according to the salvation which Jesus causes and reveals. The question then becomes: what are the ultimate insights and values that Jesus reveals as this salvation?

Jesus Himself was aware of the question of salvation. During Jesus' lifetime the rabbis played a game. They tried to summarize the whole Jewish law, the means of salvation, in the time they could remain standing on one foot. We even have examples of this in the Gospels. Various people came to Jesus to ask Him what they must do to fulfill the will of God and attain salvation. Some rabbis refused to play this game because it was dangerous. In such strict circumstances one could easily omit very important matters. However, Jesus was not afraid to try it. Recall the very compact answers He gave -- "Love God completely and your neighbor and yourself likewise." In connection with one of these episodes Luke includes the parable of the Good Samaritan, which reveals that the neighbor to be loved is anyone whom we meet who is in need.

Without standing on one foot, and aware of the possibilities of over-simplification, I shall try to sum up what the Church is as an instrument of salvation. My definition is as follows.

The world is related affectionately to God as to a dear and loving Father, whose effective desire is that we exist. God is the world's beyond. We exist to be the enjoyment of God's friendship and partnership. When sin compromises our existence, God does not destroy our existence or allow it to be destroyed. He continues to give. So, our being or existence is both given and forgiven, the gift of God. This is what Jesus reveals

to us about God and his Church which reveals
the savior God.

Such a compact definition needs detailed explanation
which the rest of this chapter will provide.

God: Father and Forgiver

Jesus uses a special word, Abba, to describe His,
and our, heavenly Father. This is a term of endearment
and affection, rooted in children's familiar speech,
and is well translated as "Daddy." God is described
as Father, we as His sons. This is not intended to
keep us in a state of perpetual minority as children
all our lives. Nor is it a sexist device to exhalt
males and demean females. Rather, God is called Father
to emphasize that our origin and existence is not merely
the result of cosmic forces. We are neither accidents
nor tricks nor playthings of the gods, nor are we
abandoned by a hit-and-run sire. We are sons. In the
language of the ancient world, son was the term that
designated the full dignity and status of the child
and designated the young person as the successor and
heir to the parent. Hence, Father and Son language
is by no means a denigration of a human being. It is
rather, the strongest assertion of human dignity.
Obviously the word Father is used here in its best
sense -- the one who makes it possible for those who
are incapable of being and living on their own to be
and live. The Father is one who causes new life and
then takes care of it. In this sense, God can be
thought of equally well as a Mother. God is not sexist,
nor should our theology of God be so.

As both Creator of the world and its sustainer,
God is its Father. He is also Father insofar as He is
the forgiver of the world gone astray and fallen. Ever
since the Fall of Adam and Eve, God has enabled the
fallen sinner to survive. God seeks out His fallen
creatures and remains a grace to them. They are clothed
in the favor of His presence. Throughout the entire
Old Testament, which is a history of the Broken Covenant, God remains faithful to His faithless spouse,
the chosen people. This faithfulness reveals God's

ability not only to create, but also to cure. God's care of the fallen creature shows that God is redeemer as well as Creator. The grace of both creation and redemption enables God to be the Saving Father and Mother of the human family.

Humanity and Divinity -- Question and Answer

What is the fundamental option of being Catholic? We have just read it. We, as Church, are the witnessing, explaining, and practicing community of this Savior God, this God who sustains and forgives us. We can put it another way by explaining the Savior God as our "beyond." All philosophy and all religion know that there is something beyond our limited experience. The Greek philosophers called this "beyond" the apeiron, but they did not agree on what this apeiron is. Sophisticated philosophers are not the only ones who know that there is an apeiron of some sort. We all experience this sense of beyond in our very normal everyday lives. There is something beyond us. It is there before we are born and after we die. Its existence cannot be denied. To deny it is to affirm it in the very denial.

So, the only serious question is, what is this beyond like? Asking this question is not an option for us; it is part and parcel of our very being. It is why contemporary German philosophers call the human being the Seinsfrage. Sein means being, to be; Frage means question. Hence, by our very being -- not because of any particular action or experience -- but by our very being we human beings are the question, "What is it all about?" This is the being that Hamlet expressed when he asked "To be or not to be, that is the question." Karl Rahner, a famous Catholic theologian, is even more emphatic. He asks, "What do we mean by man? My reply stripped to its essentials, is simple: Man is the question to which there is no answer...we are still a question to which we can give no answer on the basis of our own lives. Man is the unanswerable question." Does this lead to out-and-out cynical skepticism? Not really, because the Christian is very wary of all the quick and easy answers that are proposed to life's

problems and ultimately to the problem of life itself.
Some of these "quickie" answers, unfortunately, also
come from within the Church. That does not, fortunately, make them right. The only true "answer" is ultimately the God who saves us by loving us and enabling
us to love Him in return. The beyond is not a dark
and empty abyss, but the boundless mystery whom Jesus
called "Abba, Father" (Mark 14:36). W. H. Auden expressed it beautifully when he wrote:

> That after today
> The children of men
> May be certain that
> Father Abyss
> Is affection
> To all its creatures
> All, all, all of them
> Run to Bethlehem. (W. H. Auden, For The
> Time Being, 1944)

Does all this have anything to do with the Church?
Yes, indeed, everything. What is the Church really all
about? It is the memory and the tradition of Jesus in
the continuing history of the whole world. Jesus is
God's answer to the questions which we human beings
not only ask in individual inquiries, but are in our
very lives. Grammarians may wince, but how much more
striking that last sentence would be if we wrote it
this way: "Jesus BEs the revealed answer to that question which we human BEings BE by the very fact that we
BE at all." Why all this emphasis on BEing? Because
Christianity claims to be the answer to all our questions -- not just some, but all. This is why we prefer
the word "to be" to all others. Thus, God is the
answer to our basic being. He is our beyond. Jesus,
in turn, was the explicit answer of God to our explicit
question. And the Church, as the sacrament of Jesus,
is His answer to us. Question and answer are God's
gift.

The Church and the Trinity

Recently, theologians have re-emphasized an old
understanding of God which had gotten lost. The
economic (or salvation history) Trinity is the imminent

136

Trinity. What does this opaque language mean?

Abstractly it means that Jesus revealed God to us in history just as God is in Himself. Concretely it means that Jesus revealed God as Father, Son, and Holy Spirit. God is not only this way in regard to the world outside Himself; His very own being is a personal communion. In their attempts to explain this, theologians use words like one nature, three persons, relation, trinity, and triune God. This is all very complicated theology, and fortunately we do not have to go into detail here. We shall treat only those aspects which contribute closely to our understanding of the Church.

There are several legitimate theories "explaining" the Trinity. These options have been accepted within the Church as long as they don't violate two conditions. First, they may not divide the ONE God into THREE gods (tritheism). Secondly, they may not reduce the fullness of the THREE-personed God to the level of ONE person (monist or monarchical monotheism). Such explanations would end up making God no more than a created, human person -- perhaps Superman or Superwoman -- but nothing significantly greater than or different from us. This would mean that the "Beyond" would be only more of the same. Our only options, then, would be either pantheism or atheism.

The Church has always insisted that any explanation of the God revealed in the New Testament must include the equivalent of one divine nature and three persons. These words are not necessary, but the meaning and points they are intended to make must be present, whatever language and concepts are used.

Of all the Church's doctrines, the Trinity may be the most practical. It emphasizes that "to be" is "to be related to one another." The revelation of God as Father, Son, and Holy Spirit is the simultaneous revelation that God's very own being is being-with. Since the human world is in the image and likeness of God, human being is also being-with.

The use of abstract terminology about the Trinity has only one purpose -- to show that in the triune God

137

"being" is revealed as communion and communication. God is God only because He is simultaneously Father, Son, and Holy Spirit. God is Father only because He is simultaneously Son and Holy Spirit. In a recent article Karl Rahner wondered whether many people understand the Trinity by dividing one God into three parts and then calling these parts the three persons of the Father, Son, and Holy Spirit.

Clearly this would be a false way to understand God as Trinity. The true understanding is that God is one God in three different persons simultaneously. There is no first and second, no before and after. God the Father, the Son, and the Holy Spirit are immediately with each other and for each other. Only thus do they -- and can they -- exist at all.

In understanding the Trinity one begins to understand the nature of the Church and the world that it is part of. First of all, this understanding means that by His very nature God can be with us and for us. Since it is God's very own nature to be for and with, it is "natural" for Him to be able to be with us. His very own being is communion with us.

The communion and communication of the divine with the human happens in Jesus. The creed emphasizes that Jesus is truly God and truly man, truly divine and truly human. Dogma and theology have emphasized that this truly human and divine Jesus is only one. To describe this oneness in Jesus theologians invented the term hypostatic union. This term means that Jesus reveals the perfect compatibility, the perfect congeniality of divinity and humanity. Indeed, Jesus not only reveals, He is this perfect congeniality.

To describe this perfect congeniality theologians invented the term perichoresis. It comes from two Greek words and literally means to "dance around together." It means that in Jesus the divine and human are so happy with one another that they have to dance with one another. This idea presupposes that dancing is a sign of being pleased with one's partner. One need only observe couples at a dance to understand that dancing together is an expression (a symbol, a sacrament) of being pleased with and enthusiastic about one another. <u>Perichoresis</u> has also been used to describe the relationship of the Father, Son, and Holy Spirit: They are so happy with one another that they must dance with one another. This divine dancing spills over into Jesus, who embodies the dancing of the divine and the human.

What has this to do with the Church? Again, the answer is everything! The Church is the special sign and agent of God's congeniality with His creatures. This is what Vatican II meant when it described the Church as the "universal sacrament of salvation." Salvation includes what we can distinguish as creation, grace, redemption, and glory. All these words are ways of describing degrees and historical stages of God's self-communication to what is itself not God, the creation. Vatican II elaborates: "By her relationship with Christ, the Church is a kind of sacrament or sign of intimate union with God, and of the unity of all mankind. She is also an instrument for the achievement of such union and unity." (<u>The</u> <u>Church</u>, #48).

The Church is not primarily a moral obligation or set of laws that we must obey, nor is it primarily an organization. Instead, it is the answer to the question, "What's it all about?" The answer is God, whose sacrament is Christ, whose sacrament is the Church. Christ as Sacrament tells us that the BEing of God BEs for us. The Church as Sacrament tells us that this Christic BEing of God for us is not limited to the historical Jesus; through the Holy Spirit this power of God is available for all ages. The sign of this availability is the disciples, the Church.

As sacrament the Church is the symbol and agent of God our savior, who wants everyone to be saved and reach full knowledge of the truth. This does not make the Catholic Church an exclusive sect of those few privileged ones who are in the know, while everyone else is mired in the morass of sin and stupidity. The Church is not an elite of the privileged. Like its founder and source, it is a sacrament of service -- of

God and of the world. To emphasize this Jesus washed
the feet of the disciples and asked "Do you understand
what I have done to you? You call me Master and Lord,
and mighty; so I am. If I, then, the Lord and Master,
have washed your feet, you should wash each other's
feet. I have given you an example so that you may copy
what I have done to you." (Jn 13:13-25).

As sacrament the Church is to imitate Jesus.
Jesus was not greedy and selfish about His perichoresis
with God. Indeed, He "was divine... he did not cling
to his equality with God; he emptied himself to assume
the condition of a slave and became as men are; and
being as all men are, he was humbler yet, even to accepting death, death on a cross (Phil 2:6-8). Jesus is
the fullest symbol of God in the world. His own enjoyment of God precisely motivated Him to share God with
others. In traditional terms this is called grace.
In the chapter on Worship we will see that the grace
of Christian living involves both liturgy and ethics.

Church -- Witness of Christ

The Church is the witnessing sacrament of the
faith which is rooted and revealed in Jesus, the perfect congeniality of God and humanity. Mission, liturgy, and ethics come together in the Church in a trinitarian unity. A practical consequence of this unity
is that each and every member is fully responsible for
the Church's witnessing. Obviously, it would be impossible for all to witness in the same way. Even Jesus
didn't do everything. Our witness is not rooted in a
particular office or role, but in the faith which is
shared by all.

This faith describes the entire trusting relationship of the creature to God. It excludes nothing
except sin; it includes everything except sin. Our
mission as witnesses involves not only sacraments and
sacramentals, preaching and Bible, public and private
worship. It also includes our ordinary everyday lives
lived in faith, hope, and charity and our social action
for the reform of the world's ills. Witness involves,
among other things, constructing churches and factories,

having and baptizing babies, practicing medicine and growing food, playing and praying. As St. Paul insists (1 Cor 10:31-33), whatever we do, we are to do it in such a way that Christ is visible in our lives and shared with our sisters and brothers.

Definitions of the Church

A way of further understanding the mission of the Church and its meaning for us is to define it, but attempts to define the Church are difficult because the Church is connected with God. God is incomprehensible and cannot be defined. Thus we must use images and metaphors to describe the Church. R. S. Minear has discovered over 80 different images of the Church in the New Testament. Although these all fit togther to form an organic whole, they are not all equally important, so we shall restrict our examination to just a few.

People of God

The Church, as the People of God, demonstrates that through creation and in spite of sin, the world belongs to God.

God will never reject us because we are His. As Hosea (2:24) the prophet emphasizes, God says to us even when we are sinners, "I will love the unloved; I will say to No-People-of-Mine, you are my people, and they will answer you are my God." As the People of God we are not homeless and wandering. We have roots, and we know where they lead -- to God.

To call the Church "The People of God" also emphasizes two important dimensions of the Church. First, it shows that we are not absorbed into an infinite, impersonal deity as some religions teach. Grace does not destroy us as persons. It elevates us to friendship with God.

Secondly, the image stresses the family character of the Church: baptism and confirmation constitute the faithful as a brotherhood, a single People of sisters

141

and brothers. We must constantly remind ourselves of this, for there has been a strong tendency to divide the Church into two parts.

This may be seen in what the historian Congar refers to as the hierocratic tendency in which the Church came to be identified with the clergy. In fact, the Church became identified with the hierarchy, and the clergy's celibacy and increasingly monastic life-style during the Middle Ages supported this equation. Both their clothing and housing next door to the church building separated them from the normal life of society. This identification of the Church with the hierarchical priesthood affected its symbolism tremen-dously. The Church was seen less as the sacramental sign of the whole world being saved and more as a particular place, a building, which was a refuge from the world. The old Greek idea of the temple as a special place cut out and separated from the world pre-vailed, instead of the new Christic understanding of the Temple as the whole world becoming the full adult mystical body of Christ.

The obscuring of the Church as the sacrament of God's friendly treatment of the world in Christ has negative results for the inner life of the Church as well as its mission. The less the Church is identified with the whole people and the more it is concentrated chiefly in some members, the less it is inwardly the brotherhood desired by Jesus and thus becomes less effective as the sacrament of Jesus. That is why the Church must be so careful to avoid all elitism and grasping for power. The Church is not a privileged sect; it is the whole People of God. Within the Church there should be no sects. The option of being a Catho-lic enables us to regard and treat all human beings as our brothers and sisters. That is the meaning of the Church as the People of God.

Mystical Body of Christ

Other images of the Church also emphasize this brotherhood and communion. One of the most popular has been the Church as the mystical Body of Christ. "Mys-tical" has frequently been used to distinguish this body

of Christ from the historical body of Jesus in
Israel and the sacramental body of Jesus in the Eucharist. This image is acceptable as long as care is
taken not to let the Church fade off into some vague,
unreal, unhistorical "mystical" experience.

The Church is not a perfect body, one which would
exclude the failures and the sinners. Mystical Body
emphasizes the intimate, intense union of Jesus, the
Friend of Sinners, with His Church -- even His still
failing, sinful Church. The Last Supper discourse of
Jesus in the Gospel of John emphasizes our communion
with God in Jesus and His Church. He is the vine, we
are the branches. The Church is the Mystical Body of
Christ because we share His life. St. Paul's focus
is on the local Church community as a charismatic
community. Many different, mutually supporting members contribute to the identity of the Church as the
Body of Christ. In the Epistles to the Ephesians and
Colossians the focus is on the whole, universal Church.
These are not contradictory approaches which exclude
each other. The first emphasizes the mutual relationship of each member of the body to each other; the
second the relationship of these mutual members to the
Body's one head, Christ.

Spouse

The Church is also described as the Spouse of
Christ and of God. This image comes from the Old
Testament prophet Hosea. The term spouse is applied
to both God as husband and Israel or Church as wife.
Although God is regarded as the male spouse and the
Church as the female, nothing is taught about the rela-
tive dignity of men and women. Actually, the image
tells us more about God than about the Church.

It tells us that the relationship between God and
the world is neither a business, professional, nor a
client-centered relationship. God's relationship with
us is what we hope marriage will be -- lasting, supporting, warm, tender, affectionate, and intimate. In both
the Old and New Testaments, God has been revealed as
the utterly faithful, patient, and long-suffering

spouse. So faithful is Jesus that He is even willing to die _for_ His spouse, the Church, even when it is still sinful. What the image of spouse tells us first and foremost is how much the Church is loved by God.

Tradition of Christ

Our final "definition" of the Church is that it is as the Tradition of Christ. This title also has roots in the New Testament. In the First Epistle to the Corinthians, St. Paul illustrates the idea of tradition perfectly when he says, "For this is what I received from the Lord, and in turn passed on to you (11:23) and "I taught you what I had been taught myself..." (15:3). Tradition describes that which Jesus received from His Father and gave to His immediate disciples, and what these disciples in turn gave to later ones. We are the latest, but not the last, to participate in this "handing on." What do we receive and hand on? Jesus.

This is clearly stated in the first quote above, for what Paul received was the Eucharist. Jesus is the mediation of God's eternal, transcendent saving will in history. At one time He mediated through His historical body; not He mediates this same incarnate saving will through His mystical body.

Since the Protestant Reformation many Catholics and Protestants have opposed Gospel and Tradition as if they were mutual enemies. This debate has two sources. The first is the sinful history of the Church. The handing on, or tradition of the Gospel, has in fact been obscured. The second is Luther's pessimistic view of history and his equally pessimistic tendency to equate tradition with abuse. He did this because he focused on particular traditions and pious practices which were often suspect. However, in its full and proper meaning, tradition should not be contrasted with the Gospel. As a contemporary Lutheran scholar, Krister Stendahl notes, scripture _is_ tradition, a special _amount_ of tradition set aside in a special way.

The Church as Tradition emphasizes our continuity with the historical Jesus. The Creed reminds us of this. In it we profess our belief in the Apostolic Church. This Church of the Apostles is our mediator to Christ, our connection with the real Jesus of history. This is also the import of Apostolic Succession. The apostles and their hierarchical successors are not lords over our faith, but guardians of the tradition. But we too are all guardians and bearers of this tradition.

Some years ago, Marshall McLuhan attracted much attention with his contention that "The medium is the message." This is a perfect description of the Church as Tradition -- the whole tradition, not just the hierarchy, or the Bible, or even just the sacraments. All these elements are important, but their importance must not obscure the importance of the people, the faith-full members of the Church. The WE of the Church, The Holy Spirit, and the people are the tradition. The handing on of the Good News, the Gospel of Jesus who is with us always to the end of time, has been entrusted to us. WE must make disciples of all the nations.

The Catholic option means a commitment to Jesus as the special sign and agent, the sacrament of God's saving will. This commitment requires that we enjoy this salvation and participate in the mission which shares it with all people. Only after we have made this commitment and chosen this fundamental option may we ask about further and more particular options. Grace does not destroy nature but presupposes and builds on it. As the society of grace, the Church expands and elevates the natural possibilities and capabilities of humanity. We need to give up nothing truly human or natural in order to be Christian and Catholic.

In fact, the Catholic tradition has been all embracing. The authentic Catholic spirit is universalist, as the very name suggests and requires. Thus Cardinal Newman could say, "They (Protestants) are ever hunting for a fabulous primitive simplicity; we repose in Catholic fullness." Yves Congar and others have described Catholicism as the search for plenitude

and fullness, Protestantism as a passion for purity.
Protestantism has also tended to emphasize "either-or"
and "alone." Thus, it speaks of faith alone, of grace
alone, of scripture alone. It speaks of faith or
works, scripture or tradition. On the other hand,
Catholicism has emphasized "both" and "and." Both
Karl Rahner and Hans Urs von Balthasar speak of the
"Catholic and." The latter notes that Protestants
are suspicious about this "and," which belongs to the
very kernel of Catholicism. He then explains that this
Catholicity is rooted in "The Catholicity of God...
because by His very nature God is catholic and because
in Jesus Christ and ultimately in the Holy Spirit this
Catholicity of God has opened itself to the world."

Both hasten to warn that this Catholicity does
not mean simply piling up tons of options in a completely undifferentiated manner. It enables the
Catholic Church through life and teaching to differen-
tiate and choose the best available options. Thus it
can represent most fully that divine fullness of which
it is the anticipation and pledge, the sacrament.

The Church: Universal, Particular, Local, Domestic,
Person

This universality of options is implied in the
description of the one Church as domestic, local,
regional (particular) and universal. In fact, there
is even an ancient tradition which describes the
individual believer as a or the Church. In recent
centuries attention has been focused on the universal
Church, especially as it is represented by the Pope in
Rome and the Roman curia. Our Church has become the
Roman Catholic Church. Such concentration is not
absolutely wrong. Every group of people has to have
a center about which it gathers. But such concentration can also have bad effects, especially when it
leads us to ignore or devalue the Church as regional
and local.

Without any hesitation at all the New Testament
refers to the family or house community as the Church.
What we would today call a parish or a diocese or even

146

a national conference of dioceses is also called Church. For example, St. Paul speaks of "the Church of God in Corinth," "the churches in Galatia," and "the churches of Asia" (1 Cor 1:1; 16:1). Even the Epistle to the Colossians, which emphasizes the cosmic Church, still speaks of "the Church which meets in her (Nympha) house" and of "the church of the Laodiceans" (4:16). According to Yves Congar, the Apostles and the older theologians all emphasized that every individual believer is the Church.

Why is this? Clearly, not to foster pride in the individual or conflict among the various churches. No, it is because the basic idea of the Church requires it. The Church is the communion of humans with God and with one another. This is why even the individual Christian can be and is Church. Of course, individuals as such do not exhaust the possibilities of the Church. Therefore, the Church is also actualized in communities.

Church is, then, universal, particular-regional, local, domestic, even personal. Unfortunately, the New Testament only lists these churches, and leaves the explanation of why they are a Church up to us. Let us first indicate explanations which are not adequate. The universal Church is not composed of pre-existing independent units of the pre-existing universal Church. The relationship of the churches is similar to the relationship of the divine persons in the Trinity. As all three persons are one God simultaneously, from the very beginning, so are all the individual churches the one Church. Of course, like all comparisons, this one limps, but it is still more correct than not. We can say that the Father, Son, and Holy Spirit are the expressions of the divine nature. Likewise, we can say that all the churches (from personal to universal) are the expressions of the Church's nature.

The crucial question, then, is about the nature of the Church. One major error in answering this question is to locate the whole Church in the Pope alone, the other churches flowing out from him as from their source. In contrast, Cyprian, an early Church father who died in 258, emphasized that the origin of the Church's unity is the Father, Son, and Holy Spirit.

Part of the difficulty stems from the fact that the Pope wears many hats. He is the Bishop of Rome, Primate of Italy, Patriarch of the West, and Pope of the Universal Church. As the history of the Church shows, it is very easy for the decisions made by the Pope as Bishop of Rome or Patriarch of the West to flow over onto the rest of the Church. However, such decisions may not have universal validity. Furthermore, what might be legitimate as a local inspiration can easily become inappropriate for the universal Church. This requires no conspiracy on the part of the Pope and certain Church officials. It is simply a consequence of the influence inherent in the Pope's position at the center of the universal Church.

Anti-Rome?

Now, all this is not to induce or further any "anti-Roman complex." There has been enough anti-Roman propaganda on the part of non-Catholics, and Catholics alike.

Our purpose is to demonstrate that the adequate appreciation of Church in all of its manifestations clearly requires that we put into perspective the recent emphasis on Rome. We can certainly live and practice being the Church more effectively if we have this appreciation that our families, local parishes, dioceses, and selves are the Church, each in its own proper mode. These modes are not interchangeable. Each has its own unique and irreplaceable value and role to play in keeping the memory-tradition of Jesus Christ alive and flourishing in history.

Why can this be? Because the Church is primarily the assembly of those who accept Jesus as the special revelation of God, enjoy this grace-gift, celebrate it in sacrament, proclaim it in word, practice it in faith, hope, and charity, do it in ethical social action and share it with the whole world in every possible way. This can happen in Mid-Town, U.S.A. as well as New York City, in a family house-church as well as St. Peter's Basilica, in the humble service of brothers and sisters as well as a solemn ecumenical council. It can happen right here and now, across the world. It happens in the individual person who lives a life of faith, hope, and charity in the utter ordinariness of everyday life. Jesus' life was also ordinary -- so ordinary that people thought they could refute and reject Him because He was only a carpenter's son.

Because the Church is the sacrament of the world's salvation, it must be respectful of the natural, cultural, and psychological attributes of the people who constitute it. There always has been a pluralism in the Church -- grudgingly conceded, sometimes energetically enjoyed. There also has been an undeniable tendency toward colonialism in the Church. Practically, being Christian/Catholic involved being Western, too. In fact, at least since the Gelasian Decree of 495 there has been a tendency to emphasize the "Roman-ness" of the Church, symbolized by the introduction of Roman into the Creed. Again, to say this is not to be anti-Roman. It is to remind us of the dangers of "cultural imperialism," which would ignore or even suppress the "genius and tradition of local cultures," as Vatican II said. One way of celebrating the memory of Christ and being His tradition would be imposed on all people and cultures.

Many middle aged Catholics can remember when they were told that Mass was always said in Latin, everywhere and by all people. Such assertions were well-intended, but wrong. Even when people were making these statements, Mass was also being offered in the languages of the Eastern Rite Churches. Latin may have occupied a special place in the history of the Church, but it is not a sacred language compared to which other languages are secular. All languages are just as able to express the memory of Christ, to bear His tradition.

Cultural pluralism is still alive in what are called the rites of the Church. There are fewer now than there used to be, and they are still not fully appreciated. But they have survived and clearly will do so in the future. What is a rite? It, like the Church itself, is not easy to define. Basically, it is a particular group of people who have a particular way of being the Church (in a particular place), but always in unity with the whole Church. This "particular way" includes liturgy, law, devotions, theology, spirituality, music, and art. "Particular place" is in parentheses because geographical location is no longer nearly as important as it used to be. Long ago a rite really did tend to be located in a particular place, but travel and migrations have scattered members of these rites all over the world. Americans who live in cities like New York, Philadelphia, Pittsburgh, Cleveland, Chicago, Gary, San Francisco and others could be familiar with these rites. Their church buildings look different from Western ones and are identified by different names -- Greek, Ruthenian, Byzantine, Russian, Serbian, Maronite, Ukrainian. As their names indicate, these rites were originally located in the Near East, Eastern Europe, Russia and India. As they've become dispersed across America with immigrant groups, though, these rites experience special problems because of the conflict between the modern urban American culture and the old-country culture in which their liturgy is still celebrated.

About 18 rites are officially recognized in the Church. Other Western rites which once existed were simply overwhelmed by the Roman rite, the one that is predominant in the United States. It is possible to transfer from one rite to another, although some legal technicalities are required. This is an option that should be considered, especially by those who may like the more ornate liturgical experience that some rites provide. These rites also present other options. For instance, priests of the Eastern rites are allowed to be married, although this right was suppressed in the United States in 1929-30.

As these rites struggle to survive in a new cultural situation, it is possible that other rites are struggling to be born. Although the forces of centralism are still strong, there is also a strong movement toward greater recognition of local groups and their own particular cultures. Worldwide, but especially in Latin America, there is the phenomenon known as comunidades de base. This term does not translate well, but the usual translation is base or basic communities. What the term means is well-expressed by this definition: "homogeneous groups of eight to forty Christians who share common interests and values: where on-going relationships predominate and who view themselves as an ecclesial unit." Any single such community would not be considered a rite. It is not unthinkable, though, that a larger group of these would want to join together for certain common interests. This would not, of course, require nor should it result in the dissolution of the small units themselves. That would be to fall prey to the same malaise which the base communities were supposed to heal. The great advantage of these communities is that they take seriously the local nature and dimension of the Church. They are not necessarily separatist. They could be, of course, but, then, so can anything. These base communities are one of the bright spots on the current Church scene precisely because they understand and practice that the Catholic Church of Christ is truly present here and now in this group of people.

What is needed today is greater recognition of this truth, not only in official rites or in base communities, but in the entire pastoral activity and theology of the whole Church. Again, no plea is being made for anarchy, chaos, or caprice. The greatest possible diversity is to be nurtured within the unity of the Church. As the officials of the Church, the bishops must be alert so that they don't close off legitimate options. So we, the members, must be alert lest we encourage or permit them to do so.

Some options in the Church have been provided by the mobility our automobiles give us. The ability to go to one Church instead of another is clearly a desirable option. By now it should be clear that "going to another parish" is not merely catering to one's whims. It is being the Church in a particular way at a particular place and time according to the cultural and personal pluralism God Himself has provided. As the Church is not confined to consecrated buildings, so it is also not confined to legally and geographically apportioned units. The options provided by local

151

mobility can have salubrious effects beyond one's individual self.

Peter Berger, a Protestant and a sociologist, said that (Roman) Catholicism is like a Baroque rococo basilica -- filled with an exuberant profusion of images, statues, paintings, and art of every kind in every nook and cranny. In comparison, Protestantism is like a Calvinist church -- stark, plain, denuded down to the bones. The comparison is good. Partly because of its huge size the Catholic Church has more options to offer to more people.

The Church is coming more and more to take seriously what Pope Pius XI said: "Men were not made for the Church, but the Church was made for men: for us, men, on account of our salvation." This means that the "Church" must take us more seriously precisely where it finds us. For salvation happens not in a universal vacuum, but in this real world. Karl Rahner has suggested that the Church did take a giant step in this direction at Vatican II. He contends that this council marks "the transition of the Western Church to a world Church... a break such as has occurred only once before, that is, the transition from Jewish to Gentile Christianity." In this "third epoch" of the Church's history, the full glory of God's universal saving will in creation and Church can be brought into sacramental visibility and fulfillment throughout the whole world, with all its personal and cultural diversity.

To succeed in this option of true Catholic plenitude, the Church will have to be more option-al and option-full than ever.

QUESTIONS

Personal Reflection

1. When you are with other Catholics, do they seem full of life?

2. Have you ever felt close to God when you are with other Catholics?

152

3. Was your father a good example of God the Father? Your mother? How could the image of God described in the text help them? How could it help you to be a better person?

4. Name ten people you feel close to. Are any of them Christian? Catholic? Do you think the Church is or should be like a family?

5. Do you think a person who rejects the necessity of the Pope or the bishops for Christian living should be a Catholic? What role have priests played in our life? Favorable? Unfavorable?

Group Discussion

1. Do you know any pseudo-religions? If you were not a Catholic, which religion would you choose?

2. Is the Catholic Church the only way to be religious? The best way? Is it like a family?

3. What is the best way the Church can help us? Of everything discussed in this chapter, which do you feel was the most significant for understanding the Church?

4. Of all the descriptions of the Church discussed here, which do you think is the best one? Which is the one most of the people you know would approve of?

5. Of the various options of theology given in chapter three, which would you say this author favors?

Review Questions

1. Explain the statement: "The first option is basically Which, not Whether." Is the Roman Catholic Church the only church?

2. What does it mean that Jesus and the Church are to bring us full life?

153

3. What is Jesus' relationship to the Church? What
    does it mean to say Jesus is our salvation?

4. Explain the summary statement of what the Church is.
    (p.

5. What is the relationship of the Trinity to the
    Church?

6. List and briefly explain all the definitions of
    the Church the author uses throughout the chapter.
    Do these apply to all the Christian churches?

SUGGESTED READINGS

Congar, Yves
Lay People in the Church
Paulist, 1967

Surveys the history
of the theology and
the place of laity
in the Church.

Dulles, Avery
Models of the Church
Doubleday, 1976

Examines different
ways people live their
understanding of
"Church."

Keating, Charles
Community
23rd Publications, 1977

This collection of
practical essays
examines the theology
of the Church as
community.

Kress, Robert
Christian Roots
Christian Classics, 1978

A portrayal of the
Church as a community
of saints and sinners,
not an elite sect.

McBrien, Richard
Catholicism
Winston Press, 1980

An easy-to-read com-
prehensive survey of
Catholic thought and
belief.

Minear, Paul
Images of the Church in the
New Testament
Westminster, 1960

Traces the continuity
of the theology of the
Church in the New
Testament.

Rahner, Karl
Theological Investigations,
vol. 6
Seabury, 1974

A collection of essays
on the Church, showing
how the concept of
Church relates to a
pluralistic and secular
world.

Schnackenburg, Rudolph
The Church in the New
Testament
Herder and Herder, 1958

Examines the doctrine
of the Church as it is
found in each book of
the Bible.

VII. OPTIONS IN LEADERSHIP

ROBERT KRESS

Leadership in the Church is a difficult topic because it is a complex one. For instance, under "lead" the unabridged edition of the <u>Random House Dictionary of the English Language</u> has 54 items plus four synonyms and one antonym. The single antonym is "to follow." Under the four synonyms are included escort, precede, persuade, convince, excel, outstrip, surpass, head, and vanguard. These give some idea of what a leader does or is. At the same time they clearly illustrate how diffuse the idea is.

An additional difficulty afflicts the topic of leadership in the Church. For a long time <u>the</u> model for Church government and leadership was the monarch. Many theologians supported the idea that Church government is monarchical by divine law, which means that Christ established the form of a monarchical regime in the Church by immediately conferring supreme power on Peter alone. Others shared this power only through Peter or the Pope and in dependence on him.

In this view the Pope rules the whole Church. He allows the bishop to rule over a small part of this Church, and the bishop allows the pastor to rule over an even smaller part. The mood and the mode of this ruling is really and truly monarchical. This mood carried over into religious communities which were originally intended to be brotherhoods and sisterhoods. The "leaders" of these communities quickly became not only Father Abbot and Mother Abbess. They also became priors and prioresses, new patriarchs and matriarchs. The same mood also prevailed in marriage and family life. Where the Catholic male spouse was not only husband and father, he was also head and often enough king. The throne may have been as threadbare and plain as Archie Bunker's chair, but throne it was.

156

None of this implies that the male monarch in Church or home was necessarily brutal or oppressive. He may have been kind, gentle, and wise. However, he was the leader, THE BOSS. He exercised his leadership as monarch. In the Church THE BOSS was the Pope.

Although the theory continued to proclaim that the Church was a monarchy, it was really an oligarchy ruled by a few privileged and powerful insiders who were found, for the most part, in the Roman Curia. Power to legislate, judge, and carry out laws governing the Church was concentrated in this small group of Pope and Curia.

Leadership in the Church: Power in the Holy Spirit

According to St. Paul, "everybody has his own particular gifts from God" (1 Cor 7:7). Since these gifts are from God and are really the Holy Spirit and since the Holy Spirit is God's power, all Christians have the power which makes authority and leadership possible. This is clear in the New Testament.

> There is a variety of gifts but always the same spirit; there are all sorts of service to be done, but always to the same Lord; working in all sorts of different ways in different people, it is the same God who is working in all of them. The particular way in which the Spirit is given to each person is for a good purpose. One may have the gift of preaching with wisdom given him by the Spirit; another may have the gift of preaching instruction given him by the same Spirit; and another the gift of faith given by the same Spirit; another again the gift of healing through this one Spirit; one, the power of miracles; another prophecy, another the gift of recognizing spirits; another the gift of tongues and another the ability to interpret them. All of these are the work of one and the same Spirit, who distributes different gifts to

157

different people just as he chooses (1 Cor 12:
4-11).

We have here the raw material for a proper understanding of leadership in the Church. The social psy-
chologist George Herbert Mead, provides us with the
tools to shape this raw material into a coherent theory.

Mead was interested in the formation of human personality through the interaction of the individual with
the greater society in which the individual exists. He
said:

> This relationship of the individual to the
> community becomes striking when we get minds
> that by their advent make the wider society
> a noticeably different society. Persons of'
> great mind and great character have strikingly
> changed the communities to which they have
> responded. We call them leaders, as such, but
> they are simply carrying to the nth power this
> change in the community by the individual who
> makes himself a part of it, who belongs to it.
> The great characters have been those who,bby
> being what they were in the community, made
> that community a different one. They have
> enlarge and enriched the community. (<u>Mind</u>,
> <u>Self</u>, <u>and</u> <u>Society</u>, ed. C.W. Morris, 1962)

First, we must note that Mead distinguishes between "great minds," "leaders," and "genius" on the
one hand, and all the individual members of the community on the other. Even more noteworthy in his
statement is that these "leaders" are only doing in a
greater manner what every member does just by being a
member. In the Church, member does not mean passive.
That is the point of New Testament texts such as the
Epistle to the Hebrews, which emphasizes that "in the
whole Church everyone is a first-born son." In the
Biblical context, this statement means that everyone
has power.

Insofar as leadership means making the community
in which we live different, we all have what is

essential to leadership. Members of the Church are not merely passive objects of the hierarchical leaders, nor is the Church a pyramid in which everything filters down to the base, the laity, from the point at the top, the Pope. Neither is the Church a democracy or even a modern, centralized, bureaucratic state.

The Church has its own unique order and, consequently, its own unique leadership. This order is basically a communion whose fundamental principle is diversity in unity. In this Church there are various focal points of unity, not merely one. These points of unity are, furthermore, not for the sake of lordship or domination.

The basis of the Church's order is the <u>triune</u> God of Christianity. In the past, emperors tried to use the doctrine of monotheism to reinforce their imperial and totalitarian claims. The Church used the doctrine of the Trinity to refute them. The emperors focused their claims on the one God as Father, Creator, and Lord of the world. In contrast, the Church emphasized the relationship of the Church and the whole world to all three persons of the Trinity and emphasized the Holy Spirit. For example, according to St. Augustine the unity of the Church of God is the proper work of the Holy Spirit. This society of the Church, which makes us the one body of Jesus, belongs to this Spirit. (<u>Sermo</u> 71, co 20. P.L. 38:463)

The Church's trinitarian source enables and requires it to be a communion. In the previous chapter, we emphasized that the Church is a WE -- the one person of the Holy Spirit in the many persons who are the members of the Church. Our share in the power of the Holy Spirit is part of our Church-life. Our roles in the Church, which are given to us in the many gifts of the one Holy Spirit, are also shares in the power of this Spirit.

We can and must, therefore, conclude that every member of the Church is properly, not merely figuratively, a leader in the Church. As Mead indicates, and as sacramental theology has long implied, being baptized gives one a role in carrying on the memory and tradition of Christ. Theology has regarded Confirmation as the sacrament of active participation in the Church's life, Baptism as the sacrament of receptive membership. Yet even the receptive status of the baptized infant is already a share in the Spirit's activity whereby the Church is built up and brought to perfection. Not only the Pope, then, not only Cardinals, Bishops, and Priests, but all are active in the Church and thus all are leaders. For all enlarge and enrich the community, thus making that community a different one than it would have been without them.

Of course, some leaders will be more outstanding, as Mead indicates. Their leadership will be at least more striking and more visible, whether more charismatically like Mother Teresa of Calcutta, more prophetically like Sister Teresa Kane of Washington, more intellectually like Karl Rahner, or more hierarchically like John Paul II. This line-up is not meant to be exhaustive, but it still reveals something very interesting. All four are priests and religious. Does this counter my emphasis that the Holy Spirit empowers and activates all the members of the Church and not just some? No, there is a very practical reason for the predominance of clergy and religious. Usually, they are the only ones supported financially and otherwise to devote themselves to those matters visibly identified with the Church.

These four people are good examples of what we called leadership in the narrow sense, those Mead calls "great" or "genius." Nevertheless, in the Church we all have the ability to be leaders because we have at our disposal the resources of the society of the Church, and the powerful gifts of the Holy Spirit. Only by artificially restricting our resources to ordained Church offices could we limit leadership in the Church to certain kinds of executive authorities.

Consequently, we would be doubly remiss to allow leadership in the Church to be restricted to the hierarchy. In practice many people expect these hierarchs to provide __all__ leadership in the Church, but the hierarchy may be neither personally capable nor sacramentally empowered and commissioned to do this. The proper functioning of hierarchical leadership in the Church can be insured only if we appreciate all the different kinds and modes of leadership. From the beginning through to today the Church has had differentiated membership. We should appreciate the structural leadership we have, and we must be diligent in guarding it against abuse and in promoting its healthy service in and to (not over) the community. We should also refrain from overloading it by requiring the ordained leaders to do everything. Ordained leadership is not the only nor the most important form of leadership in the Church.

Holy Orders and Order in the Church

If Church leadership is not supposed to be concentrated exclusively in a few clerical hierarchs, what is the clerics' proper and precise role? The scriptures indicate that their function is to keep order in the Church. There is a special gift called __kubernesis__. Its basic meaning is governing, but it can also be translated as administering or regulating. There is, then, an office and a gift whose function is to provide for the good order of the Church. Some people are empowered by the Spirit to govern and administer. They mediate among all the various gifts given by the Holy Spirit so that the Church is not a chaotic scandal but an orderly witness to God's grace. This was certainly a great concern of St. Paul, not only in regard to the very enthusiastic and charismatic Church at Corinth, but to all churches. This still describes the role of executive, authoritative, hierarchical leadership in the Church. Its primary concern is the coordination of the diversely gifted members of the Church. Ordained leaders are truly and properly managers, administrators (as long as this term is not restricted solely to building management), and coordinators of the Church and the Church's life. As such, they are the pastors and the shepherds of the flock, but not dictators of the flock or the faith.

It is interesting that we spontaneously speak of the sacrament of the priesthood. Strictly speaking, there is no such sacrament. The Council of Trent speaks of the "Sacrament of Order," although it immediately describes it in terms of priesthood. However, even here the context emphasizes the priest's role in the order of the Church. It is also interesting that one is ordained when one receives this sacrament. This is not to reduce the ordained priesthood to merely a function. Rather, it is to emphasize that the chief function of those who are ordained is to provide for the order of that community of which they are members. Their first and greatest dignity is to be members of this Body of Christ, not officials within it.

Other words in the New Testament also indicate that the ordained enjoy a managerial, coordinating role within the Church. The Greek word for bishop is episcopos. Its basic connotation is overseer or superintendent. Another word in the New Testament is proistamenos, which could be translated foreman: the one who stands in front and is thereby able to see over and also go before (lead, guide). The Germans use the word vorsteher (before-stander or stander-in-front-of) to designate the leader of a community or a presider at the liturgical assembly. In the chapter on worship we speak of the ordained priest as presiding officer. The advantage of this language is that it does not insinuate that the ordained leader is above or over the congregation.

Pope, Bishop, Priest, Deacon

For a long time the ordained ministry in the Church has been divided into three grades or degrees: Bishop, Priest and Deacon. (The Pope is regarded as a special kind of Bishop.) Such a division is acceptable, but it is not absolute. It is not absolute because the three offices themselves have been described in various ways. The power which each confers has been expanded or contracted according to the needs of the Church. In our own century, for example, the power to confirm has been extended from the bishop to "simple" priests. Furthermore, we now have special or extraordinary ministers of Holy Communion.

The proper understanding of ordained leadership, ministries and offices in the Church is hindered by a Biblical fundamentalism on the part of both Catholics and Protestants. The latter tend to demand that everything be absolutely explicit in the text of the New Testament. They do not find much about ordained ministers there, especially not Catholicism's Pope, Bishop, Priest, and Deacon. Catholics tend to find that everything necessary to prove that these ordained offices do exist is so clearly present in the New Testament that no one could deny it. These are tendencies. Both are inadequate, since they both tend to ignore that grace does not destroy nature. It presupposes, builds on, and perfects it. Human nature is a social and political nature. Hence, human beings must live together in order to exist and flourish. In order to exist and flourish together they must organize themselves in some way or other. All societies manifest various kinds of leadership, into which they distribute their power, resources, and responsibility. Since the Church is composed of human beings, it must also and inevitably have institutional authority. This understanding of grace building on nature is the proper starting point for appreciating authority and leadership in the Church. Let us examine the Church's understanding of leadership as found in scripture.

The whole Church is aware that it has received power from Christ. From the very beginning there was a differentiation and specialization among the disciples of Jesus. Everyone did not do exactly what everyone else did. Later on, when the conditions required it, the Church expanded and included others in certain functions of authority and leadership. This is the significance of the account of the Seven Deacons (Acts 6:1-6), who clearly were not deacons according to the present practice of the Church. The election of Matthias to replace Judas and thus bring the Apostolic College to its required number of Twelve is also important as an example of how the Church exercises its power. Furthermore, "presiding Elders," Presbyters or "deacons" of some sort have been in the Church from the very beginning. Even Paul, the great Apostle of freedom, recognized them. Their presence is also widely reported in the pastoral and universal epistles.

Whatever may have been their detailed job description, there were clearly stewards of the tradition in the early Church. Some were more charismatic and creative, others more institutional and conservational. There was, then as now, the possibility that authority would become fascist, leadership totalitarian. Judging from New Testament exhortations against lording it over others and treating them as if they were subordinate subjects rather than brothers and sisters, it is clear that the desire to dominate others has been a problem from the very beginning of the Church.

We have spent so much time on institutional leadership and official authority in the Church for two reasons. First of all, it is important in itself. As a community of human beings, the Church must organize itself as well as it can. Institutional officers and leaders can make or break an organization, and concern for this proper organization is as old as the New Testament itself. St. Paul urges it in the First Epistle to the Corinthians when he declares that the Church must be orderly "since God is not a God of disorder and confusion but of peace" (14:33). This orderliness is apologetic and missionary, and is designed to make the Church attractive to nonbelievers. It is also spiritual, for it is to support those who are already members of the Church in their practice of holiness. Such orderliness is impossible without institutional authority and official administrators.

We have also spent so much time on this kind of leadership to show that it does not have to be restricted to the smallest possible number. In the history of the Church, official authority has been arranged in different ways. Hence, the present structure of Bishop, Priest, and Deacon is neither univocally clear nor absolutely unmodifiable. New ways of distributing the hierarchical and administrative power of the Church can be searched out and created. History, as well as theology, clearly indicates that such change can come about if there is both the necessity and desire for it in the Church.

Grace as Authority: Leadership of the Faithful

In spite of the tendency of Church authority to concentrate itself in institutional offices, history shows that leadership in the Church has never resided solely in the ordained hierarchy. The leadership of so many saints is also a strong confirmation of the theology of leadership we are advocating. This theology correlates leadership with the diverse gifts of the Holy Spirit which enables all members of the Church to enlarge and enrich the Church.

Another idea developed by G. H. Mead can further our understanding of leadership. Peter Berger sums up Mead's theory of the "significant other" thus.

Probably the most penetrating theoretical account of the process is the one given by Mead, in which the genesis of the self is interpreted as being one and the same event as the discovery of society. The child finds out who he is as he learns what society is. He learns to play roles properly belonging to him by learning, as Mead puts it, "to the role of the other" - which, incidentally, is the crucial sociopsychological function of play, in which children masquerade with a variety of social roles and in doing so dis-cover the significance of those being assigned to them. All this learning occurs, and can only occur, in interaction with other human beings, be it the parents or whoever else raises the child. The child first takes on roles vis-a-vis what Mead calls his "signifi-cant others;" that is, those persons who deal with him intimately and whose attitudes are decisive for the formation of his conception of himself. Later, the child learns that the roles he plays are not only relevant to this intimate circle, but relate to the expecta-tions directed toward him by society at large. This higher level of abstraction in the social response Mead calls the discovery of the "general-ized other." That is, not only the child's mother

expects him to be good, clean and truthful,
society in general does so as well. Only
when this general conception of society emerges
is the child capable of forming a clear conception of himself. "Self" and "society," in the
child's experience, are the two sides of the
same coin. (Introduction to Sociology, 1963)

The significant others are leaders. They are not
only Pope, Bishop, Priest, Deacon, not only Monks and
Nuns, Brothers and Sisters. The significant others are
all those who, empowered by their gifts from the Holy
Spirit, enlarge and enrich the communion of their
Church.

We should be encouraged, then, to expand participation in all kinds of leadership in the Church. More
and more members of the Church should be brought into
even the ordained, hierarchical leadership. The purpose of this expansion is not to clericalize the
Church even more, but to declericalize it. In our
everyday graced lives of faith, hope, and charity we
are all already significant others in action and in
sign. The further inclusion of as many members as
possible in as many public official signs of the
Church's life is basically desirable.

There is a precedent for this in what is described
by the technical theological term "reception." It is
not widely known. The historian Yves Congar suggests
this definition: "By reception we understand the process whereby an ecclesial body truly makes its own
(appropriates) a determination which has not originated
within itself. It does this by recognizing in the
measure promulgated a rule which is in accordance with
its life." This definition takes seriously a traditional axiom of the Church that says, "What concerns everyone should be dealt with the approved by everyone."
Reception does not demand, for example, that the decisions of an ecumenical council be submitted to a subsequent vote of ratification by all the members of the
Church. But it does mean that the relationship between
the council and the Church is not simply one of "above
and below." The life of the Church is not merely one

of obedient submission of some members to the superior authority of some others. The Spirit of God has been poured out on all. The <u>reception</u> of this Spirit makes us all <u>active</u> in the Church.

There is a parallel to the receptive role of the disciples in the founding of the Church and institution of the sacraments by Christ. Not only Jesus had to act. So did the disciples. Otherwise, what Jesus had done would simply have evaporated. The "reception" by the Church gave social and historical body to the actions of Jesus. Therefore, Jesus also had to take the disciples into consideration when He carried out His mission. Their receptivity inevitably entered into His activity. Likewise, in the later Church the receptivity of all the faithful enters into the activity of the hierarchy. It is an essential condition of the hierarchy's activity and efficacy. Unfortunately, we do not yet have many concrete structures in the Church to facilitate this interplay between the initiatives of the hierarchy and the reception of the Church at large.

Effective and practical ways to enable the Church's communion to be a real communication are still lacking. An ecumenical council has some value in enabling the Bishops to communicate with the Pope, but a council is necessarily an occasional occurrence. As soon as the Council Fathers leave Rome, the Roman Curia resumes its hegemony. Complete reform of the curia has been promised for centuries, but is still not complete. At other focal points of communion the communications system is not much better. Diocesan councils are often too cumbersome and time-consuming. Communication, which takes place on a personal, individual basis, has difficulty overcoming the dangers of clericalism and cronyism. I realize that the factual history of Diocesan and parish councils has not been one of outstanding performance. Their suppression, however, hardly seems to be an adequate solution. Overcentralization is an accusation often leveled against Rome; it is equally applicable to diocese and parish.

The monarchical, pyramid model of the Church in which everything comes down from above is not conducive to good communications within the communion of the Church. A much better directional metaphor would be inward and outward. As we have seen, there are various focal points of unity and concentration within the Church: Pope, Bishop, Local Pastor, diocese, and parish. Inwardly, these points emphasize unity. Outwardly, they emphasize mission. In no way do they emphasize superiority. Hence, Church authorities must learn to govern other than by unilateral decree from above. Their gift of kubernesis has not made then monarchs and dictators, but ministers and leaders. This new style of governing must be discovered, since no ready-made models are available from either the political right or left. Not only old-fashioned monarchists can afford to be dictatorial and clerical. Such clericalism can come from the left as well as the right. In the so-called "New Equality," Robert Nisbet (Twilight of Authority, 1975) also detects a "clerisy of power" in "the long succession of philosophers and intellectuals" to positions of institutional leadership in society and government.

Leadership and Holiness

The chief way of being a leader in the Church is through holiness. All other modes of leadership are secondary and subordinate. Since Catholicism is a Way of Life and Holiness, guardianship and stewardship will be most intensely exercised in the form of holiness. This holiness enables even those who are not hughly placed executive leaders to have enormous authority. St. Catherine of Siena (1347-80) is an example of such leadership. She was a saint who mixed fearlessly in the world and spoke with the candor and authority of one completely committed to Christ. At the same time, she was a young woman with no social position who was accused of hypocrisy and presumption by Church officials. Fortunately, though, she was vigorously defended by the Dominican religious order with which she was affiliated. Her efforts resulted in Pope Gregory (1370-78) returning the central administration of the Church from its Avignon exile (1309-77) to Rome. She was proclaimed a Doctor of the Church in 1970. Her life reflects all the necessary components of leadership: a command of the resources of society, prestige, competence, responsibility, and action.

Catherine of Siena illustrates the truth that holiness is a prime mode of leadership in the Church. A good way to study leadership in the Church is to study the lives of the saints. Of course, there are many saints who are not celebrated by name, rank, and number. That is why we celebrate the Feast of All the Saints. The purpose of this feast is to give all of us nameless people encouragement, inspiration, and consolation.

We celebrate some saints by name. We do this because of their unique grace, because they are sources of encouragement and inspiration, and because they present concrete models of leadership -- holiness in the Church.

Thus there are female and male saints, young and old, poor and rich, dumb and smart, unschooled and schooled, black, brown, yellow, red and white, married and unmarried, lay and religious, recluse and reformer, activist and contemplative. As such, saints do not have to be the most emotionally balanced and pleasant people one might hope to meet. We can hope that they would be, but they need not. Saints show us that what any particular age regards as "normal" need not be required for holiness, sainthood, and leadership in the Church. Oddity is not a sign of holiness, but neither is it a sign of unholiness. The Portuguese proverb, "God writes straight on crooked lines" is also applicable here.

Saints are concrete examples of holiness in the world. They are the many various "personal sacraments" of the many, various gifts of the Holy Spirit. As they live their gifts in the concrete history of the world, they become little sacraments of the great sacrament of the Church, the sacrament of the world's salvation. They are thus leaders even though many do not occupy high places in the official structure of the Church. The saints also have an auxiliary function. They take away our favorite excuse: how could "poor lil ole me" be expected to be a leader in the Church, a saint?

From Abraham and Sarah through Zachary and Mary to the
Disciples of Jesus, the response has been the same:
"For God everything is possible." In and through the
little people of the world and the Church, God's power
is effective and manifest in the world and the Church.
Saints are the embodiments of God's grace which has made
all of us "significant others" -- leaders in the cosmic
liturgy of grace and salvation.

Conclusion

There is only one Shepherd to whom the sheep belong. That is God. His son Jesus is the good and
chief shepherd, the only gate to the sheepfold. Jesus
is our leader in faith and salvation not because He
was an ordained priest with executive power and authority, but because He said God, here I am! I am coming
to obey your will. Jesus' leadership has not made Him
a dictator who lords it over others, but rather the
"first-born of many brothers." In Him we are all
"first-born sons and citizens of heaven." As such we
must all commune and communicate as brothers and sisters ministering to one another. The power-full gifts
of the Holy Spirit make us too leaders, not as dictators, but as "significant others" in the Body of Christ
to whose Father alone one may be subject.

QUESTIONS

Personal Reflection

1. Do you think you are a leader? State three reasons
   for your being a leader; three against.

2. What do you plan on doing five years from now? Can
   the Church help you be there? Should it?

3. How will you contribute to the betterment of humanity? Name three contributions you have made.
   Three that you can make.

4. How would you like to influence others? Try to
   influence one person this week.

5. A leader needs vision. What is your vision of a good life? What is one action you can do regularly for the next three weeks that can help you fulfill your vision of the good life?

Group Discussion

1. Name five people you consider a leader. Are any of these religious leaders? Do religious leaders differ from secular leaders? From leaders in business or government?

2. Does one become a leader when he or she is elected or appointed? When do we know someone is a leader?

3. Name three religious leaders. Who are their followers? Where are they leading their followers? Is it worthwhile to follow religious leaders? What are the consequences? How do you know they are doing a good job of leading?

4. What are the qualities of a good Church leader? Should a Church leader try to influence governmental policies regarding war, business, pollution, equal rights, and economics?

Review Questions

1. Name three difficulties in discussing leadership in the Church.

2. What is the Church's unique leadership and order?

3. Explain these statements. "Those in the hierarchy are leaders." "But leadership cannot be restricted to them."

4. What is the purpose of leadership as found in those dedicated to keeping order in the Church?

5. How are saints leaders? How can you prove through scripture and sociological argument that they may be accepted as leaders in the Church?

SUGGESTED READINGS

Brown, Raymond
Priest and Bishop
Paulist, 1970

Shows the biblical origin and basis of hierarchical office in the Church.

Coleman, William, et. al.
Parish Leadership Today
23rd Publications, 1979

Offers practical hints for church leadership by people on the local level.

Drucker, Peter
Management
Harper and Row, 1974

The theory and practice of leadership and management by one of the nation's management experts.

Kress, Robert
Whither Womankind
Abbey Press, 1975

Examines the role and status of women in the Judeo-Christian tradition, putting special emphasis on the ordained and non-ordained ministers.

Power, David
Various Gifts: Lay Ministries in the Church
Word Books, 1981

Shows the past and present ways of being active in the Church without being ordained.

Rademacher, William
The Practical Guide for Parish Councils
23rd Publications, 1979

Surveys the problems, practices and solutions of organization at the grass roots.

VIII. OPTIONS IN WORSHIP

ROBERT KRESS

A hundred years ago a German philosopher, Friedrich Nietzsche, told us that people will build altars in the temples of their hearts if they find the altars in the temples of their churches unsatisfactory. A few years ago an American sociologist, Peter Berger, told us that people need ritual if they are to be able to live together.

In this chapter we are going to think about the altar and the ritual which surrounds it in the Catholic Church. The "altar" is <u>where</u> we worship; ritual is <u>how</u> we worship. In general, worship means how we respond to what we think is important. Worship is connected with adoration. In worship we adore what we consider to be the most important thing in our lives. This "thing" is usually called God.

As soon as we hear the words worship and ritual, we probably think of the Mass. We think of the altar with candles, crucifix, missal, chalice, bread, wine, and water; the priest and servers in special clothing; the movements from place to place with genuflections, bows, hands folded, and arms extended. There may also be a choir singing special songs. Even the building where the Mass is held is special. There are steeples, stained glass windows, and decorations depicting God, Jesus, Mary, Saints, and various symbols from the Bible and the later history of the Church. The congregation has its own ritual actions. People bless themselves with holy water when they enter the Church. They sit, stand, kneel, and sing at designated times. They shake hands with one another or give some other sign of peace.

We are also familiar with the worship and ritual of other sacraments and devotions. These all involve

173

special actions such as processions and anointings and special materials such as water and oil. Some devotions involve special seasons, for instance, the way of the cross in Lent, the rosary in May and October, the advent wreath before Christmas.

Ritual and Worship

Before we go into more detail about Catholic worship and ritual, we would do well to consider how ritual and worship exist in our daily life without denominational trappings. As I write this, we are in the midst of a special ritual season. We are just finishing the regular football season and preparing for all the Bowl games of the Christmas season. Shortly we shall be celebrating Thanksgiving, Christmas, and New Years. What does all this have to do with ritual? Everything. All these events involve ceremonial celebrations of what the people involved think is important. We all have levels of importance. Some things are important, others more important, still others most important. There is eventually one single thing which alone is most important. This used to be called G-O-D. Our response to God is called worship in the strict sense. We shall examine this in detail shortly.

We respond to the things we regard as very important in two ways. One way is our ordinary daily life; the other, special ceremony. One example of something very important in our lives is our national identity and, therefore, our political duty as citizens. The first way we respond to this very important thing is in acting as responsible citizens in our daily lives. We try to live lawfully, change bad laws, promote justice and combat injustice, and make our society a better place to live. We vote, pay taxes, and educate ourselves.

The second way is more symbolic and not something we do every day. This way involves special ceremonies and special days. Some examples are the laying of the wreath on the tomb of the Unknown Soldier and ceremonies at other cemeteries on Memorial and Veterans Days and the singing of the national anthem, especially on national holidays when we celebrate our nation's identity. Of these days the most important is the Fourth of July, but there is also Labor Day, Washington's and Lincoln's birthdays, Columbus Day, and Memorial Day.

Living our daily life well (ethics) and gathering with others in ceremonial action (worship) are complementary. Both are needed if human life is to express itself fully. That is what Jesus means when He says "If you are bringing your offering to the altar and there remember that your brother has something against you, leave your offering there before the altar, go and be reconciled with your brother first, and then come back and present your offering" (Mt 5:23).

Examining ritual more closely we find that it is the outward and visible action by which we express our inner attitude. Often we do this spontaneously, as when we cheer when our team scores the winning basket in the final seconds of a basketball game. The winning players dance about excitedly and pat each other on the back in an immediate, spontaneous, external expression of their inner happiness. Tragic events also call forth similar immediate external reactions.

However, there are also external expressions of our internal thoughts which are not spontaneous, but planned. This is what we usually mean by ritual or rite. A ritual is a particular way of doing something. It is a symbolic action and usually is communal, thus involving more than one person. For example, a kiss is an action in which two pairs of lips make contact. This action can be more than just physical touching, however. It is often symbolic of the love between the two people. Some symbols are natural and spontaneous. For instance, a smile is a symbol of happiness, fire of smoke, clouds of moisture. Others are deliberately and rationally developed, but even these usually have a natural basis. Of course, symbol can be falsified. Thus, the kiss Judas gave to Jesus was not a symbol of his friendship, but of his betrayal. Misuse is possible, but it does not ruin the whole practice of symbolic actions. We cannot live without ritual or without symbols.

175

We need and use ritual because we are human beings.
Our ritual is sensible and sensual because human beings
are bodily and have senses. We express ourselves, our
very being, in these sensible rituals. For example, a
handshake is not only an external designation of friendship, it also makes us friends and can increase our
friendship. A kiss is not only an external designation
of our love like a label on a suit. It is, rather, our
love itself. In the symbol of the kiss our love becomes even more loving.

Symbols are important because the relationship
between the thing symbolized and the thing symbolizing
is much more intense and intimate. So, we call the
kiss a symbol of love. For husband and wife sexual
intercourse is a symbolic act of love and a symbol of
their marital union. Here, we can recall immediately
the relationship between ethics as everyday living and
liturgy as the symbolic, ceremonial celebration of this
life. Sexual intercourse as the act of love and symbol
of marriage can hardly be expected to thrive if the
daily life of the husband and wife is filled with warfare.

Remember that ceremonies, rites, and "liturgy" in
the wide sense are not restricted to the strictly
religious. They belong to human nature. We use sensible actions to profess and celebrate what we think is
important. I once took a friend to the finals of the
Indiana State High School Association basketball tourn-
ament. He could hardly believe his eyes. Everyone
was dressed in their school colors, not only the high
school students themselves, but their parents, grand-
parents, baby brothers, and sisters. Their cars and
buses were also decorated with these colors. And
frequently they even decorated the highways between
their hometowns and Indianapolis, where the games are
played. Can you imagine this intensity for the fencing
team or the debating team or the home economics club?
When I ask this question, I am not passing judgment on
the intrinsic value of these activities. I am only
pointing out that human beings surround those activities
which they deem more/most important with special ceremonies and rituals.

176

One could wonder whether ritual is all that important in regard to the really important things of life,
such as our relationship to God. Our answer has two
parts. First, all traditional religions have rituals.
Some are very simple, others are very elaborate.
Secondly, even those people who do not have a traditional religion or believe in a traditional God have rituals. We need only to recall May Day parades in Moscow
and Havana, the ceremonials of secular humanist organizations, graduation exercises in schools, the rituals
of nature worshippers or occult practitioners. We can
safely conclude that ritual is a true and characteristic dimension of human experience. Everybody has
rituals.

Now we must deal with our second topic. Is it
legitimate for human beings to have "altars" for worship? Does everybody have not only rituals in general,
but also a ritual of worship? Is it natural for all
human beings to adore someone or something? This is
important here because the purpose of our Catholic
liturgy and ritual is worship. Our ceremonies are
concerned with what we think is absolutely most important -- God. Put another way, worship is an act of
religion. So, our question about the legitimacy of
worship boils down to the question about the legitimacy
of religion.

Does everybody have a religion? Yes. This does
not mean, of course, that everyone is a Catholic or a
Lutheran or a Jew or a Muslim or a Buddhist or a Hindu.
So what does it mean? It means that all human beings
and societies do in their own particular way what
Catholics do as Catholics. That is, they organize
their lives, individually and socially, on the basis
of values and insights which they perceive to be ultimate. This is called the anthropological or sociological definition of religion. It passes no judgment on
the goodness or badness, the truth or falsity of the
religions. It simply says that this is how human beings do, in fact, live. We can observe such a religion
in their lives.

In this definition "organization" is the equivalent of the ethics and liturgy we spoke of regarding ritual worship. "Values and insights" refer to that which philosophy calls the good and the true. "Ultimate" refers to that which we have customarily called God. Even those who strongly reject a belief in God have a god. They may not have God in the traditional sense, but they do have a god of some sort. Why? Because in their lives there is a truth and a good which is ultimate. It is final. One cannot go beyond it and find a still greater good and truth. In their lives this ultimate good and true plays the same role as God plays in ours. One can even be expected to become a martyr, to give up one's life and die for this ultimate good and true.

We can say that everyone has a faith or religion. An incident which the well-known German philosopher, Max Muller, narrates about himself illustrates this. When he was a young and eager philosophy student, he went to the university chaplain and told him that he couldn't believe all this "Catholic stuff" anymore. The chaplain replied calmly, "That's all right. If you don't believe this, you"ll believe something else, and probably much worse."

These introductory comments enable us to see that an option is NOT whether we want to have ritual, liturgy, religion, and worship. Our option concerns only what kind of ritual, liturgy, religion, and worship we want. In fact, our option is really about God. What kind of God do we worship?

The Adorable God

In some religions, worship tries to make contact with the gods (or god). In others, it tries to make the gods become present in this world. In still others it tries to placate angry gods who are bent on hassling the human race. None of these applies to us. For us God is always present. What others think they must seek and strive to find is already present. Our worship is the enjoyment and celebration of this already present God, this God who freely gives Himself to us.

God: Creation and Communion

Worship is primarily and principally based on the relationship of the worshipper to the worshipped. For us in the Judeo-Christian tradition this means that worship is rooted in the positive likeness of the creature to the creator. In fact, it is rooted not only in likeness and external resemblance, but in communion with God. That is what creation means. Creation establishes the Godly and not-godly to intimate communion. They are with one another: partners, friends, lovers. Only because creation creates this communion is redemption even possible, not as a correction of the creation, but as a healing of the creature whose misbehavior has compromised the original communion.

Worship of God does not have to presume or promote an inferiority complex on the part of human beings. Quite the contrary! It emphasizes the dignity of human beings, for it acknowledges the communion of God with humanity. In a sentence, worship is our (ritual) celebration of our faith's understanding that the ultimate value is not against us, but for us. God in the book of Genesis creates us to walk with Him in the garden of paradise. When we turn this garden into a desert by our sin, God does not chop off our legs. Nor does God annihilate us nor take away the gift He gave in creation. He does not abandon or reject His sinful creatures or hide from them. They hide from Him. But God searches them out and promises them a redeemer. For us, worship is the acknowledgment and celebration that God is both the giver and forgiver of human beings. God does not make being human impossible. Even when human beings compromise the creation by sin, God still enables them to survive and flourish.

The Friend of Sinners

Even our sins do not make God desert us. God still takes the initiative, as he did with Adam and Eve, Cain and Abel, and Noah. Later on, when the chosen people sinned, it was not God who deserted them

179

but they who deserted Him. At least they tried to break
the covenant between themselves and God. But God's
loyalty and love are so strong that He kept the covenant alive.

In Luke's gospel Jesus told us parables about the
lost sheep, the lost coin, the lost son. Unfortunately,
we too often emphasize the "lost-ness." The emphasis
is instead on the seeking shepherd, woman, and Father.
The parables emphasize that these three take the initiative. They stand for God who always takes the initiative. We call this divine initiative by various names
-- creation, grace, redemption, salvation, forgiveness.
Clearly the parable of the prodigal son is a misnomer.
It is precisely the parable of the forgiving Father.
The Father is the central figure, not the errant son.
Too often sermons let the Father's action begin only
when the son is almost home. That is entirely wrong.
According to the text, it is precisely the Father's
presence in the son's memory which enables the son
to even think about going home.

Jesus emphasizes that He does nothing on His own;
He does only what He sees the Father doing. He is the
sacrament of God who is His and our Father and Mother.
In this world, therefore, Jesus also takes the initia-
tive in being with sinners. As the sacrament of God
His Father, Jesus is the "Friend of Sinners."

We can safely conclude that our understanding of
God makes it both possible and fitting to worship God.
We do not worship a tyrant, a grouch, a penny-pincher.
Rather, in the words of Dante, the poet, we acknowledge
God as the "happy or joyous maker of the world and
human race."

Faith and the Sacraments of the Faith

We must always retain this unity between our faith
in who we believe in and worship, and how we celebrate
this faith. Unfortunately religious instruction and
practice have not always kept faith and worship together. As a result accusations of superstition and magic
are levied against the Catholic theory and practice of

worship. However, in more than 20 years of pastoral and teaching experience I have never met a Catholic who thought that sacraments were magic.

The sacraments are not magic. They do not make God do something God doesn't want to do. The sacraments are symbols of what God is already and always doing. They are the practical, effective symbols of our faith that God wants everyone to be saved. Through the ritual ceremonies of the sacraments we proclaim salvation, the good news of Jesus Christ.

Jesus: Priest and Sacrifice

The whole ritual of the Christian religion comes from Jesus Christ's priesthood. We are accustomed to associate priesthood with sacrifice, and rightly so. Therefore, it is critically important to understand sacrifice properly. Sacrifice has been a key term in the history of religion and worship, but a proper understanding of it is not easy. It has been excessively, if not exclusively, connected with sin and slaughter in the minds of our contemporaries. This is not a good connection.

Worship is the acknowledgment and celebration of our relationship with God. As we have seen, our relationship to God is not based on sin. Rather, it is based on the gift giving nature of God and His communion with His creation.

If this is so, then, neither worship nor sacrifice can be the attempt to placate an angry God. In any case, we cannot compel anyone to forgive us. Forgiveness is not earned, but given. If this is the case among humans, how much more so between us and God. So sacrifice is not something we do to make God forgive us and like us. It is not primarily reparation of and for sin.

We must next ask whether sacrifice requires slaughter. Here we have to reckon with the ravages wreaked by Biblical epics in the movies and the pastel paintings in religion books. Do we not spontaneously

181

think of slaughter when we hear the word sacrifice?
An altar, a priest, a bull or sheep, or, if it's really
a grade B Biblical epic, a blond maiden! And BLOOD!
And above this scene there is usually a dark, threatening sky, clearly indicating that the gods are angry.

None of this really belongs to sacrifice. Essen-
tially, sacrifice has two basic elements: 1) the recognition of the worth of another, and 2) the affirmation
of this worth through the dedication of oneself to the
one worthy of such dedication. This dedication is
usually symbolized in some kind of action. The destruction of something, especially something living,
was one preferred symbolic action. This destruction
symbolized that the life of the worshipper, the
sacrificier, was completely dedicated to the worthy
one.

This total dedication can also be present without
the symbolic destruction of an animal. Sacrifice,
as recognition and total dedication, can take place in
one's daily life without any ritual. This sacrifice
of daily living will naturally seek some kind of symbolic, ritual expression. Nevertheless, the ritual is
not sacrifice. The Epistle to the Hebrews (10:5-7)
means this when it says: "and this is what Jesus said,
on coming into the world:

You who wanted no sacrifice or obligation,
prepared a body for Me.
You took no pleasure in holocausts or
    sacrifices for sin;
then I said,
just as I was commanded in the scroll of
    the book,
'God, here I am! I am coming to obey your
    will.'"

According to the Epistle, human beings are sacrificial
and priestly by and in their very lives, as long as
they live for and not against God. Jesus was not priest
and sacrifice only on the cross. His entire life was
priestly and sacrificial, for it was completely given
over to the recognition of God and the expression of

this recognition in His daily life. That is what "to obey God's will" means.

Nothing Jesus is or does is solely for Himself alone. He is always for us. His life reveals to us that our lives are, like His, the priestly worship of God. The sin of the world made Jesus' sacrifice difficult at times, and finally even bloody and destructive. But that was because sin is destructive and deadly, not because sacrifice is.

Since we live in a sinful world, our worship will also have to deal with sin. But, once again, sacrifice is not because of sin. Sacrifice is because we are in communion with the Father in the Spirit through Jesus. Our worship and sacrifice must never become preoccupied with our guilt and sin. Rather, they must always concentrate on God's gift and grace. Our creaturely communion with God is always the primary element, not our sinful fall and flight.

Why is Christ the perfect priest and perfect sacrifice? Not because He died on the Cross, but because He is the perfect dedication of humanity to divinity. Of course, had Jesus refused the Cross, His dedication would not have been perfect. But his perfect union with God enabled Him to undergo suffering on the Cross. The priesthood of Christ does away with the error that religion is only interior. All life is a ritual. All life is priesthood, the external expression and realization of our inner dedication to God. Secondly, the priesthood of Christ shows that all Christians, not a small elite, share in the priesthood of Christ. Christian worship is not restricted to a few moments of our lives, like the Mass and the sacraments. All of life is the ritual of the worship of God. We are not schizophrenics, split into the sacred and the secular.

The whole of creation is in, through, and for Christ. This means that the real world, as it actually' exists, is already "priestly." It has been caught up into the mediation between the divine and human which the man Jesus is. This means that worship of God is also the recognition and enjoyment of our own worth. In this real and really graced world, our lives are our sacrifices. We are both priest and victim.

There is another manner of expressing this. All of Christianity is the memory of Christ. We celebrate, keep alive, and hand on the memory of Christ in two ways. One is by imitating Christ in our daily lives of service to God and our brothers and sisters. Jesus gave us an example of this when He washed His disciples' feet and said, "I have given you an example so that you may copy what I have done to you" (Jn 13:15). This is the spiritual sacrifice of our whole life and the spiritual or universal priesthood of all the believers. At the same supper Jesus gave us another way of celebrating, and keeping His memory alive in the world. This is the ritual, symbolic sacrament of the Eucharist, the Holy Sacrifice of the Mass as we call it: "This is My body which is for you; do this in a memorial of Me.... Whenever you drink this cup, do this as a memorial of Me" (1 Cor 11:24-26). There is a special, official, ritual priesthood to take care of this sacramental sacrifice in the Church.

The difference between these two types of priesthood can be summarized in a few brief statements. 1) The two kinds of sacrifice and priesthood are neither opposed nor exclusive. Each has its own irreplaceable value and function. 2) They are not two different degrees of a common priesthood. That is, one does not become an official, ritual, sacramental priest by becoming more of a universal and spiritual priest. 3) The two are positively related, because both are visible, sensibly perceptible symbols and manifestations of the faith of the Church. The universal priesthood of the faithful refers to their grace-given ability to live their whole and entire lives as pleasing sacrifices to God. This is not the same as the celebration of the Eucharist. The fundamental act of Christian living is faith, hope, and charity. The sacraments and the Christian life do not simply coincide. This does not mean that everyday Christian practice and sacramental practice are in conflict; they are simply not identical.

Theologians have taken note of this difference
between Christian living and sacramentalizing. They
have taught that the faithful who are not ordained
hierarchical priests are able to share in the celebration of the sacrament of the Eucharist because they
have received the sacraments of baptism and confirmation. These sacraments authorize Christians to join
in the public, ritual, sacramental sacrifice. Here
again we must keep in mind the parallel and mutual
relationship between the life of Christ as sacrifice
and the Last Supper and Cross as symbolic manifestations of this sacrifice. The daily, life-long sacrifice of Jesus as dedication to the will of His Father
achieves a special intensity and visibility in both
the Last Supper and the Cross. We can see that the
Last Supper and the Cross are special signs and symbols of Jesus' reconciliation with His fellow humans
and with God His Father. We are privileged to share
in these symbols as well as the life of Christ. We
call our everyday sharing in the Life of Christ grace
or faith, hope, and charity. There are special signs
and symbols of this grace, this sharing in the life
of Christ. We call these special symbols sacraments.
They enable us to celebrate our grace in special intense and sensibly perceptive ways. It is clear,
then, that we share in the priesthood of Christ in
two ways: in the everyday way of holy living and in
the special way of sacramental celebration.

The "sacramental principle" expresses this possibility of celebrating our grace. Grace truly communicates and manifests itself in and through the sensibly
perceptible matter of creation. Consequently, ritual,
like brotherly love, is truly the exercise and practice of grace. Ritual or liturgy is not merely a tag
or a cosmetic decoration painted on an already-finished
product. It is essential to human living in the
present and in the past; before and after Jesus walked
this earth.

Sacraments of Nature, Judaism, Christianity

The sacramental principle is at the heart of the
entire Judeo-Christian tradition. From the first

185

chapter of Genesis the Bible emphasizes that there is no abyss between the divine and the human, rather, there is communion. All being is basically sacramental for all being is the limited reflection of God's unlimited and perfect being. At the same time, all created being is a sharing in the being of God. It is a natural sacrament.

This is what all sacraments basically are -- the visible means whereby God communicates His life to us and at the same time shows His will for us. The difference between the sacraments of nature, the Old Testament, and the New Testament is basically the difference that exists between everything else and Christ. Like Christ, the Christian sacraments are the fulfillment of what God has been doing all along, namely, saving us. This understanding of sacraments enables us to avoid all the hesitations that were once shown toward natural and Jewish sacraments. These other non-Christian sacraments do not threaten or detract from the special dignity of Christ. They point to it and emphasize it. By God's power they can also be the symbols and causes of grace.

All sacraments, whether natural, Jewish, or Christian, are participations in the manifestations of that one sacrament who is Christ. Christ is not the negation and destruction of the natural and Jewish sacraments. He is, rather, the culmination of God's life-giving activity. God's saving will, present from the very beginning, has been progressively revealed in what theologians distinguish as nature, grace and glory. Salvation is the history of grace, whose two dimensions we call creation and redemption. Privileged manifestations of this "cosmic history of grace" are the seven sacraments. They are the highest levels of grace in symbolic form.

The Experience of Jesus: The Origin of Church and Sacraments

How did these privileged manifestations come into being? To understand this we must look, briefly, at the origin of the Church and the seven sacraments.

God wanted to share His life and happiness with what is not God. This sharing happens and is signified in Jesus, who is the perfect sharing of the creature with the creator. Jesus has an experience of God. He really is the experience of God by the non-godly. This is what theologians insisted on when they speak of the hypostatic union and the one person in two natures in Jesus. Contemporary theologians emphasize that when God becomes other than He is in Himself, He becomes human in the generic sense. In general, this becoming human is concentrated in Jesus, where the human and the divine are in perfect communication and communion. We can, then legitimately say that Jesus not only has an experience of God. He is the human experience of God.

Jesus was not selfish. In fact, His whole being was and is for others. Therefore, He did not keep this experience of God all to Himself. He shared it with others, and to do so He had to "objectify" it. That is, He had to take His invisible, inner experience and give it visible, outer expression. We do this all the time. For example, when we love someone, we show it. We can show it in words such as "I love you" or actions such as kissing, holding hands, or giving a material present such as a ring. Likewise with Jesus. He showed, and thereby shared with us, His experience of God in words and actions. The disciples received these words and actions, preserved and applied them, and then handed them on. This objective sharing is the origin of the Bible, the Church, and the sacraments.

St. John already warned us that "there were many other signs (symbols) that Jesus worked and the disciples saw, but they are not recorded in this book. These are recorded so that you may believe that Jesus is the Christ, the son of God, and believing this you may have life through His name" (Jn 20:30-31). This statement is very important for understanding how the whole Church is constituted in its life, sacraments, Bible, leadership and government. The Church cannot be founded solely by the instituting action of Christ. The receiving action of the disciples is also necessary.

187

It is logical and legitimate, then, that the Church will regard some of the objectifications which Jesus gave to His experience of God and which He shared with His disciples as more important than others.

For example, St. Paul tells us that we are baptized into the death and resurrection of Christ. In our terms the cross and resurrection are the objectifications of Jesus' religious experience of God. Thus, although Jesus' pain drives Him to cry "My God, My God, why have you deserted Me," his fundamental trust-faith is still strong enough so that He is able to pray, "Father, into your hands I commend My Spirit." These words are the objectification of Jesus' faith.

Our faith and worship are a sharing in Jesus' confident trust, especially His commendation of His dying self to the God who is His Father. The seven sacraments are special symbolic ways in which we profess and share in this dedication of Jesus to God. They are also the acceptance by the Church of some of the objectifications of Jesus' experience of the Father.

The Sacraments and Human Experience

Another way of understanding the sacraments is to look to human experience in general rather than to Jesus' experience. This classical explanation of the seven sacraments is sometimes called the psychological explanation because it relates the seven sacraments to the seven peak individual and social experiences of human life. A few examples of how to explain the sacraments may remind you of explanations you have read or heard in sermons.

Here is an example from the thirteenth century:

Baptism for beginners, Confirmation for combatants, the Eucharist for wayfarers, Penance for prodigals, Extreme Unction for the departing, Orders for the ministering, and Marriage for those who toil.

St. Bonaventure (1217-74) uses military metaphors: Matrimony is for those "who prepare new soldiers," Holy Orders for those who bring in new recruits." During his time the Church on earth was frequently called the "Church militant" or the fighting Church.

St. Thomas (1225-74) has a similar arrangement:

Sacrament	Corresponds to
Baptism	Birth.
Confirmation	Maturity.
Eucharist	Preservation and strengthening of life.
Penance	Healing sickness for the restoration of health.
Extreme Unction	Restoration of original strength and preparation for the journey through death to the glory of heaven.
Holy Orders	Governing for the sake of the common good.
Matrimony	Continuation of the human family.

These descriptions of the sacraments became traditional. They appear in official Church documents as early as 1439 in the Council of Florence's Decree for the Armenians, and as late as 1943 in Pope Pius XII's Encyclical on the Mystical Body.

Such description is critically important, for it shows how the whole of human life and history is caught up in the saving will of God. Alone, however, it could give a false impression. Yet such correlations between the sacraments and peak human experiences can be helpful. I would like to suggest the following as a possible explanation of the sacraments in a salvation-historical mode.

Baptism: Death and Resurrection of Christ.

Confirmation: Pentecostal "Enspiriting" and "Empowering" of the Disciples of Christ to be the Church, missionary witnesses of the

189

tradition and the Memory of Christ.

Holy Eucharist: Participation in the meals of Jesus, the Friend of Sinners, with sinners. A share in the Last Supper where Jesus' priestly life-sacrifice begins its consummation. Eating the bread and drinking the wine of the Eucharist does not so much turn bread and wine into our body but turns us into the Body (and Blood) of Christ.

Penance: Being brought into the many acts of forgiveness which Christ is and which He gave to people who sinned.

Anointing of the Sick: Sharing in the health and life which Jesus, the life of the world, so generously shared with His contemporaries through physical and emotional healings.

Holy Orders: Sharing in those gifts of the Holy Spirit which provide for the good order of the Church.

Matrimony: Sharing in the goodness of God's creation through the exercise of our sexuality which shares in God's own pleasure in being with us. It is the sacrament of the marriage of divinity and humanity in Christ throughout time. It is enjoying Jesus' enjoyment of the celebration at Cana.

Sacraments: Experience of Jesus, Celebration of a Catholic Church

Our daily lives of faith, hope, and charity share the daily experience of Jesus. We are also privileged to share in the sacramental objectifications of Jesus' experience. Like His, our ordinary daily experience of the Holy Spirit has certain high points when it becomes visible in the Church. We call these higher points sacraments. They give the Church a unique, visible presence in the world. Still on pilgrimage to heaven, this world-Church will be the perfect Temple and the City of God when God will be all in all. Until then, we celebrate God's presence among us in the sensible signs of our world.

Since the whole world was created and graced by God, no particular culture or art form is exclusively privileged in the relationship of humanity to God. Hence, none has an exclusive role to play in the ritual worship of the universal Church. All cultures and all art forms are equally at home in the Church and in the liturgy.

Many are reluctant to accept the implications of this universalism. A continual temptation of the Church is to make the world not only Christian, but also Western and Roman. But there is no reason why a 20th century Nigerian should have to worship like a 16th century German. In fact, there is no reason why a 20th century German has to worship like a 16th century one. The Second Vatican Council took note of this:

> For the liturgy is made of unchangeable elements divinely instituted, and elements subject to change. The latter not only may but ought to be changed with the passing of time if features have by chance crept in which are less harmonious with the intimate nature of the liturgy, or if existing elements have grown less functional. (The Liturgy, 21)

There is a legitimate pluralism in the Church which should be favored, not fought; nurtured, not negated. Pluralism in the Church's ritual does not imply anarchy or chaos. Orderliness is needed in any religion and every Church. Unfortunately and undeniably, we are often tempted to achieve order by eliminating variety and reducing options. We forget our Catholic heritage and destiny in the celebration of the sacraments.

191

Sacraments and Prayer

From what we have said it is obvious that God's grace is not tied down and limited to the seven sacraments. This does not mean that the sacraments are trivial and unimportant. It simply means that they are not everything. They have their own particular role to play in the cosmic history of salvation and our own personal histories of grace, but they do not replace our personal faith and prayer. Of course, I am also familiar with the old complaint, "Why should I go to Church? I can pray just as well in the park -- even better." Obviously, one can pray in the park, or almost anywhere else. But personal prayer does not replace the public ritual prayer of the sacraments, just as the sacraments do not replace personal prayer.

It should be obvious by now that the Mass, for example, is not "only" prayer. In fact, I usually respond to the above objection by stating that one does not go to Mass to pray. One can pray any time, any place. Of course, one does pray at Mass. But it is a special kind of praying, and it does not make other prayer impossible or unnecessary. Prayer at Mass really presupposes the other prayer. The option is not really private prayer or public ritual worship. It is really private prayer and public ritual worship. We really are able to do both.

Public ritual does more than provide a context for prayer and worship. It also provides a means whereby our faith can be handed on. Not only the official liturgy, but also popular devotions are the means by which the tradition of Christ is able to' survive and flourish. The fundamental principle of adaptation is always the same for both: the rituals are to be arranged so that the people are able to enjoy, understand, and hand on their Christic faith, hope, and charity throughout history.

Folklore as Tradition

This "handing on" happens in many ways: through official acts such as infallible declarations and

ecumenical councils; through the research and writing
of theologians and the teaching of catechists; through
the sacred Scriptures; through the official liturgy
of Mass and sacraments; and also through the unofficial
liturgy of public and private devotions. Here we must
especially recall the popular and folklore celebrations
which we so often take for granted. We might even tend
to regard them as merely secular celebrations. Of
course, they could become merely secular if we allow
their religious dimensions to be forgotten. That would
be a tragedy, for Easter eggs and Christmas trees have
certainly been important agents in the handing on of
the tradition and memory of Christ. Furthermore,
parties after baptism and burial are both professions
of faith and handing on the faith.

Sacramentals

In this context we should also mention those bless-
ings, prayers and rituals known as sacramentals. The
sacramentals, like sacraments, celebrate the graced,
holy state of life. Through these ritual celebrations
the grace which God has already given the world becomes visible in society and history. Sacramentals
are important because they prevent us from restricting
our faith-rituals to the seven sacraments and provide
us with the easiest way to adapt our rituals to any
given age and culture.

Since the sacraments are so much a part of the
constituent elements of the Church and since they play
such a fundamental role in preserving the memory and
tradition of Christ, they will be least congenial to
modification and adaptation. This has certainly been
the case in recent centuries and probably will continue
to be so.

Options will be more readily available in regard
to the sacramentals and devotions. This applies to
both the invention of new ones and the adaptation of
already-existing ones. Priest and people should cooperate to discover the needs and gifts of their
communities. Bringing these gifts into a visible,
liturgical celebration will contribute significantly

to the satisfaction of the needs. These devotions
will not only be the living of the grace that is in
the world; they will also be its symbol.

The same applies to private family devotions.
They, too, are the coming into visibility of the grace
that God has given and is always giving us. Hence,
these devotions do not serve only the private needs of
the individual families and their members. They also
serve the public needs of the Church, for they help
keep alive and flourishing the tradition of Christ in
the world.

Since these devotions do not have the same degree
of universal visibility as the sacraments, they enjoy
greater adaptability and allow for more options. The
creativity of believers as well as their loyalty to
the tradition can flourish here.

Conclusion

We both have and do not have options in worship.
One we do not have is whether we shall worship, for
we must worship someone or something. So, the first
option we do have is which God we shall worship. A
second option we have is whether we shall worship God
as Jesus Christ did, that is, whether our worship will
be Christian. If we choose this option, we have many
more options in regard to worship. The major options
are sacraments, sacramentals, public devotions, private
devotions, personal devotions. In all of these there
are the further options of the precise cultural forms
the actual ceremonies and rituals will take. Here we
can be innovating as well as conserving members of the
tradition and memory of Christ, the Church. The cri-
terion is twofold: 1) that which enables God's grace
in the world to flourish in each member individually
and in the Church as a whole; and 2) that which allows
this grace in the world to be most visible in history
and society.

The supreme law is the salvation of people. What
best serves them and best keeps the tradition alive
and flourishing is the path we should choose. A homey

example illustrates this. As I was distributing holy communion in my home parish, a very old lady approached, her rosary wrapped all around her hands. I planned, consequently, to place the host on her tongue. But she extended her hands, smiled at me, took the host in her fingers and put it into her own mouth.

I think St. Gregory, the great liturgical reformer (540-604), would have smiled too. For this elderly lady had surveyed the liturgical and devotional options available to her and selected those which would be the most effective ritual worship of her faith, thereby giving us and the whole Church an example worth pondering and imitating.

QUESTIONS

Personal Reflection

1. A ritual may be described as an often-repeated and stylized gesture of word and action. Are there any rituals in your life? Name a group of people you regularly meet with.

2. Are you a sinner? What are some of your sins? Does God love you?

3. Do you sacrifice? How can you improve your sacrifices?

4. Have your parents brought you up as a good Catholic? Do you ever think of your baptism? Confirmation?

5. What do you do often and repeatedly by yourself and/or with others that helps you be a better Catholic? Where your rituals are, there is your heart. Where are your rituals?

Group Discussion

1. Can a person be religious without religious ritual?

2. What is a friend? How is God most like a friend? Most unlike a friend?

3. Are the sacraments magic? What is the difference? Should babies be baptized? Should a couple have to prove they are good Catholics before being married in the Church?

4. Is it possible to know how to sacrifice in the Church? How? What is the best way to find out?

5. Of the different ways of showing that the seven sacraments are part of life, which makes the most sense to you?

6. What were your worst experiences of Mass? What were your best? Do you think a Catholic must go to Mass on Sunday? What is the best way of celebrating the Mass?

Review Questions

1. What is worship? What is ritual? Can we live without them?

2. Must we adore God? What kind of God do we adore?

3. How does worship emphasize our dignity?

4. Define sacrament. Sacramental principle. Jesus as sacrament. Church as sacrament. Eucharist as sacrament. Sacramentals.

5. What is sacrifice? What is priesthood? Distinguish between the types of priesthood.

6. How did the Church and Sacraments originate? Why are there seven sacraments?

SUGGESTED READINGS

Guardini, Romano
Sacred Signs
Michael Glazier, 1981

A simple but effective explanation of symbolic actions.

Jones, Cheslyn (ed.)
The Study of Liturgy
Oxford University Press,
1978

An up-to-date historical analysis of worship as found in all Christian denominations.

Kress, Robert
"The Church as Communio:
Trinity and Incarnation as
the Foundations of Ecclesiology,"
The Jurist 36(1976) 127-59.

Explores the theological background dealing with that communion between God and humans which is the basis for liturgy and sacraments.

Martos, Joseph
Doors to the Sacred
Doubleday, 1982

A comprehensive summary of contemporary sacramental theology.

Pieper, Joseph
In Tune With the World
Franciscan Herald Press, 1973

Deals with the goodness and dignity of all creation as the necessary foundation for worship.

Rahner, Karl
Meditations on the Sacraments
Seabury, 1977

A theology of the sacraments in a popular spiritual mode.

Schillebeeckx, Edward
Christ the Sacrament of
the Encounter with God
Sheed and Ward, 1959

A classic explanation of the wider meaning of sacrament, which includes Christ, the Church, and the seven sacraments.

IX. THE CHALLENGE OF PLURALISM: OPTING FOR LIFE

NATHAN KOLLAR

The American Catholic Church is between times,
on its way to a place and a style of life which is
not clear. The American Culture, of which it is part,
is also on its way to a new way of life. Hundreds of
religions and ideologies plead for our life and our
money. It is impossible to remain neutral to their
outstretched hands, for in doing so we give support
to neutrality as a way of life. As the immigrant
pattern of church life slowly passes away as the
dominant form of religious living, there is nothing to
take its place. The American way of life itself is
shifting.

New ways of life, new ideas, new people cause the
Church new problems. As the flood of immigrants
challenged the Church in the 19th and early 20th centuries, so the flight of educated, highly mobile,
middle class people to the suburbs challenged her after
the Second World War. The challenge renewed some old
ideas and brought to light some new ones.

These old-yet-new ideas once again examined the
liturgical life of the faithful: were the celebration
of the sacraments in the tradition of Catholic worship
or were they a product of recent individualism? Were
the priest and the bishop the rulers of the Church
or servants in it? Should authority be based on knowledge and expertise or on ordination? Should the
Church include democratic institutions which recognize
some of the Human Rights evident in the American Bill
of Rights? Should the knowledge of contemporary
Biblical and historical scholars be accepted in the
way the Church reads and understands her past? How
should the Catholic live in the world?

The educated Catholic has not been afraid of
ideas. Consequently, the revolutionary thinking that
occurred since Trent outside the Church swept over the

contemporary Church with violence and confusion. Belief has become a matter of discussion and argument in a way unheard of in Immigrant Catholicism. In the midst of all this, Catholics have sought the depth of their Christianity: how do we follow the call of Jesus in this new world? There are many options in contemporary Roman Catholicism.

The old ideas face the challenge of new events in American life. There have been revolutions in ways of talking and living one's sexuality; challenges to the exercise of authority in the traditional forms of governmental and large institutions; and moral crises posed by such events as the war in Vietnam: What to do with our power and might in the face of the Third World needs and desires? How do we use our power in a moral manner? Such a dilemma is also found in America's energy and hazardous-waste disposal problems: How to deal with our environment? Finally, the shrouded sin of racism was uncovered for all to see in the '50's and '60's: How were we to deal with racism in Church, state and business?

Underlying these changes are the technological advancements which place in human hands the ability to control birth, to lengthen life, to create new organisms, to fly to the stars. Increased technological ability means increased responsibility. Now we are responsible for changing and modifying nature. Systems of ethics founded upon human limit have to deal with a technology which has found no limits. As part of an international Church, we are faced with ways of life which are foreign to our Western culture. The future growth of Roman Catholicism lies in the Third World. Africa, Southeast Asia, and South America are all on the edge of change and challenge. Should we accept the formulation of change and challenge from their world or ours?

The options of the past, present, and future are the options of the American Catholic Church. That Church, which is each one of us, tries to intelligently cope with becoming a Church consistent with its past, yet capable of helping the kingdom come in the present.

The options of the past are seen in terms of the present and the future which we create.

In the midst of societal and ecclesial change, each of us is faced with individual choices. Pluralism of life means that we have many options of how to lead our life. Yet, although there is pluralism of life, we can only lead one life and make one choice at a time. In the past many choices were forced upon us by parents, neighbors, and the common values of society and the nation. Since this is no longer the case, it is all too easy to accept life as structureless and to float from situation to situation like a blob of gelatin waiting to be molded by some outside force. But a blob is not human. To choose is human. One must opt to live.

The Importance of Choosing

You must choose to live. Your body is made for choosing: the hands reach out for food, for friendship, for fashioning the world around you; your eyes open and close, allowing you to choose to see the beautiful, the horrible, the hate or the love of others; your feet walk in one direction or another. Not to choose is to choose. For instance, to refuse to eat, listen, breathe, talk, and love is to choose to die as a human being. Choices and options are part of human life.

Yet your life is not only choosing. In many ways you are chosen. Your life is both gift (how you are chosen or live), and invitation (how you choose). There are certain givens to living. You are given a physical and psychological constitution. You have a way of speaking, thinking, believing, and interacting with others which is gift. You had no choice. This is the way you are.

This gift, these "givens," are also an invitation. Your physical and psychological constitution are there to be developed. Your culture, reflected in your customs and language, shape the way you live your life, but your mind and will may create new language and customs. Your gift is invitation.

One gift is your religion. Religion is the way you live your life in the light of some ultimate value. Most people do not ordinarily choose religion. Rather, they are born into it. Your religion in this sense is gift. It is the place from which you see the world. Your option comes in accepting the invitation. Basic to understanding these last few sentences is the understanding of "disclosure."

Disclosure is best understood by experiencing it rather than by giving a definition of it. Have you ever looked at one of those pictures where you are supposed to find five lions or some other animals in the picture? The moment when you see the animals is a disclosure. Have you ever had to solve a math problem and worked and worked on it without even having a hint at how to do it and then all at once everything falls in place and you are able to work the problem with ease? The moment when everything falls in place is a disclosure. Remember how difficult it was to find your way around the building the first time you went to school? The moment when you could move from room to room, and recognize other people, that moment was a disclosure. You live in the light of your disclosures. One disclosure becomes a basis for other ones. For instance, the disclosure that Christianity is a way of life lays the groundwork for seeing that Roman Catholicism is a way to live, which in turn sets the scene for accepting American Roman Catholicism, which in turn opens the way to making any one of the many choices for worship, belief, and morality present in our Church. One disclosure builds on another. Disclosure is an insight into reality. Two people looking at the same object may see it differently. Two people experiencing life may have different disclosures of its meaning.

Disclosure is a part of religion as it is of life. As a Christian some things make sense to you that are incomprehensible to those of another religion, for instance, that Jesus is God and man. As a Roman Catholic there may be elements of your life that cause you anxiety, for example, a papal pronouncement, which to a Lutheran results only in a grin and curiosity.

As an Irish American Roman Catholic living in Southern
Virginia you may find that some people react to you
with fear, while an Irish Protestant would not be
treated in the same manner. Life is different for you
because of your gift, your disclosure of your gift,
and your way of seeing and living life.

Disclosures do not stop at birth. Life is a
series of disclosures, accepted, rejected, and ignored.
They come as a gift containing an invitation. To live
you must choose. Your world is filled with disclosures
of how to live. To live well you must choose well.

What Conditions Choice?

The difference between a human and an animal is'
the capacity of surprise. This element of surprise
limits the ability to present an exhaustive list of
those conditions which govern choice. There are, however, four conditions which play a significant role:
other people, physiology, belief and reflection.

Others or society provide a context for choice.
You need others to exist. You influence others; they
influence you. Thus you speak the language of your
society. You sing, dance, conceptualize beauty, laugh
and hate in the manner of your culture. The ideas,
values, mannerisms, and symbols you inherit from your
society influence but do not determine your choice.
The best example of how society influences you is the
language you speak. You speak your native tongue with
ease. Yet you are constantly choosing which words to
say, how to arrange them, how to express your inner-
most feelings and ideas. There are times when you
cannot find the right word, phrase, or image, so you
may create new words to indicate your choices. So
it is with the entire culture you have inherited.

Physiological or genetic determination also indicates mental and physical limitations. Yet some
humans discover fascinating ways to implement their
wished choice: physically, humans cannot fly, and
mentally, we cannot compute quickly, yet we have
rockets and computers. There is no doubt that we are

limited by the body we are, yet because we are more than our body, we can find ways to transcend it.

Belief is those ideals which direct your life and shape your choices. If, for instance, you believe that freedom is essential to each individual, you vote for those supporting such freedom, live where you will be free, and refuse to associate with friends who limit your freedom. Belief influences your options.

Yet you know your choices are not always in line with your beliefs. When you choose contrary to your beliefs, you may be indicating that your stated beliefs are not your real beliefs. You may also be discovering that "surprise" dimension of the human personality which often finds you doing the opposite of what you say you believe. In either case, belief does influence your decisions.

Reflection is the process of making yourself aware of those structures, people, and powers that influence your life. Reflection plays a part in choice as you consciously look at society, belief, and biology to see what are the actual limits to your choice. In the light of your reflections, you make certain choices.

Opting for Life

Everyone wants to make the right choice. The difficulty is in knowing which choice is right for you as an individual and for the community in which you live. There are two extremes in making choices: opting for only that which coincides with your principles and opting only for what you feel you should choose. An "option for life" from these two positions would be seen as 1) an option to follow one's principles or 2) an option to follow one's deepest intuition. There are difficulties with both of these extreme positions.

You opt for life when you choose according to your principles. "You keep the rules and the rules keep you," is another way of stating the same approach. Thus, if the rule or principle is "Thou shalt not

203

steal," you should not steal no matter what the circumstances. If one person breaks the rules then all of society is threatened. How can you be sure of what your neighbor will do if you say there are exceptions to the rule? Grant one exception and your property will be taken by the one who makes the second exception. It is better that one person suffer to sustain the rule than the entire nation be destroyed in chaos with no rule. Thus, no matter how poor you are or how desperate for food, "thou shalt not steal."

This approach has a number of difficulties: 1) it offers no guidance when two rules conflict, e.g. not to steal and to preserve my life; 2) it exalts law over human need; 3) it makes it very easy for you to judge others while allowing mitigating circumstances in your own case. You may take what you feel is your due from your employer, but when someone else does the same you may say that it's stealing.

Opting for life may also mean opting for love; opting for doing what is instinctively the right thing. Rather than rules, intuition and sensitivity to what God wants leads you to the right choice. Although such an approach avoids the difficulties and intricacies of rules, it does not avoid social chaos and individual disintegration.

When you trust only your feelings, you soon recognize what you feel today is not what you feel tomorrow. Feelings change. Your feelings about something being right may easily override the feelings of others. The sexual experimentation of the '60's and '70's ignored what happened to children and turned its eyes away from the long-term personal destruction which may take place if the sexual nature of a person is treated like a piece of candy to be tasted and discarded if it's not always enjoyable. It is easy to forget the effects of your well-intentioned actions upon others, especially when these actions are done with sincerity. It is also easy to forget that instincts may be touched by human selfishness and greed for power.

If choices based on rules lead you to the rigid-
ity of external legalism and those based on feeling
lead you to the chaos of internal selfishness, how can
you find a way to truly choose life?

You can make choices which are life-giving rather
than life-destroying if you remember that you act as a
human person. You are conditioned by all those elements mentioned above. Thus you must take as many of
them into consideration as possible when choosing.
You create from your reflection and action a life-giving way of life out of those elements which shape the
context of your choice. Your norms for reflection
take account of this reality. Both the rational,
structural dimensions of the person must be recognized
as well as the emotional dimensions. Human beings
are whole and you cannot separate principles and feelings. In considering your way of life, you must take
this wholeness into consideration in all your reflections.

Making the Option: The Fruits of Choice

How do you know that your choices are life-giving
or life-destroying? There is no absolute guarantee of
normative principles which can be given for assuring
that all your choices are life-giving. It is possible,
however, to indicate some essential conditions for
making religious choices or options.

1. If your choice leads to an inner coherence of
body, mind, and spirit, it is life-giving. Your chosen
beliefs and ways of action should not result in your
life being reduced to only biological urges, mental
convictions, or spiritual impulses. A healthy tension
should be present as each choice begins to shape your
life. This tension is a sign of inner coherence. It
takes a while for a choice to become part of your lifestyle. During this time there is always a slight un-
easiness which, if authentic, results from your gaining
balance. A choice is good if it results in balancing
your life: your relationship to people, things, structures, self, and God.

2. If your choices result in an increasing ability to live creatively with ambiguity and uncertainty, then they are life-giving. Chaos and ambiguity are part of living, but the choice you make must enable you to deal with these creatively over a prolonged period of time. The ways of belief, worship, and morality you choose should result in your being able to deal with the present tentions in life creatively.

3. If your choices result in a continuation of your self-actualization, they are life-giving. Self-actualization is a desire to become everything you are capable of becoming. It implies progression through a sequential series of stages toward increasingly higher levels of motives and organization. You grow in confidence in making and being responsible for your choices. If you find, therefore, that in making certain choices you become more narrow in your view of the world, that you become self-centered, hostile in humor, and uniform in action, then it is obvious that the choice is destroying you and reducing your ability to cope with life.

4. If the choices result in a growth of self-giving then they are life-giving. The giving of self to serve the just needs of others -- also called love -- should result from the way of living you choose. A choice which reduces your ability to love others is destructive of an essential dimension of personhood and of society.

5. If the choice results in a growth of community, then it is a life-giving option. Your choices should result in a balanced involvement with others. There is no such thing as instant community, yet your choices should result in an increased ability to live with others. When such involvement is balanced, you are not smothered by others. There must be time for quiet reflection to consider the direction and purposes of life and time for being with others, challenging them and being challenged by them.

6. If the choice results in a deeper awareness

of the ultimate in both your life and the life of the
world, then it is an option for life. In Christian
terms, does the choice allow you to be more sensitive
to the Spirit's movement in your life? Is it deepening your life in the Father, Son, and Spirit? A
traditional way of testing whether it does is that
offered by St. Paul when he suggests that the fruits
of the Spirit are: charity, joy, peace, patience,
kindness, goodness, faith, modesty, and continency.
The evidence of these characteristics in your life
indicate that the choices you have made are good.

There are many dimensions to making the many
choices necessary for living a full religious life.
Reflecting on these dimensions as they had a part in
your past and present options can be helpful in understanding where you have been, are, and will be, but
the effect a choice has in your own life is many times
a reflection of its internal structure and its roots.
The internal structure of that which you choose should
also be examined for its ability to deal with those
constitutive elements which make up your way of life.
We have looked at the fruits of your choice. We turn
to its roots.

What To Consider in the Options Themselves: The Roots of Choice

1. Do all the choices together have inner coherence? In reviewing your options, do they make sense
or do they contradict each other? Do you find that
in matters of worship you accept change easily whereas
in morality you do not? Is there a coherence or logical linkage between the various parts of your choice
or choices?

2. Are they faithful to and accepting of gospel
values and historical realities? Does the way of life
you choose have roots in the past identity of the
Church? In the scriptures? Does the option you wish
to claim identify with the Christian tradition? Or
does it reject any urging for clarification in relationship to Christianity? If your choice is to be a
choice in and for Catholicism it must be willing to

prove itself as part of the Catholic tradition.

3. Is your choice open to other ways of thought and action? The basic nature of a way of thought is that it changes in the light of further questions. Life's mysteries are never fully explained. Any system which makes such a claim is actually taking a rules approach to choosing and is subject to the deficiencies of such an approach. If it is open to other ways of thought and action, then it is also in a continual process of clarification and examination of its presuppositions. Anyone who shares a view which is willing to grow will, in turn, share that growth.

Conclusion

A child walks into the candy store, sees bright colors, smells delightful aromas, and makes a choice. The child bites into the candy and eats it or spits it out. The results of this choice are immediately evident -- would that the results of all choices or options were so evident.

All of us may choose life's goods as the child chooses the candy: by their packaging. We may also choose by acting and reflecting. When we reflect upon the "roots," the inner structure of our possible choice, we may discern whether the choice will or will not be beneficial. By their roots we shall know our choices. Many times all the examining in the world will not help decide whether this is a good choice for us. We must act. We must try it. In living the choice we may see that the choice was not a good one. Then we must act again.

Whether we gain knowledge of our choices through root or fruit, the proof of maturity is the courage to refuse to make or continue to live those choices which are or will destroy us. Only with such courage do we choose a way of life, make options in Roman Catholicism.

QUESTIONS

Personal Reflection

1. List all the possible options present in the past chapters. Choose the best of these for you. Do your choices reflect the best way of choosing for life?

Group Discussion

1. What are the basic Catholic options?

2. Are there any options which cannot be found in the Catholic way of life?

3. Name two options which you feel are most discussed and argued about in Roman Catholicism.

Review Questions

1. What is a disclosure?

2. Describe four conditions which influence our choices.

3. Describe the difficulty of making all choices based on principle or on intuition.

AUTHORS

Leonard Biallas is professor and chairman of the Department of Theology and Religious Studies at Quincy
College in Illinois and editor of the Bulletin of the
Council on the Study of Religion. He received his
doctorate from the Institute Catholique in Paris,
France and has taught at the University of Notre Dame in
Indiana, LaSalle College in Philadelphia, Loyola-Mary-
mount University in Los Angeles and the University of
Portland in Oregon. He is the author of more than
40 articles and reviews in scholarly and popular
journals. He was vice-president of the College
Theology Society from 1979 to 1981.

Daniel A. Brown is a professor of religious studies at
California State University, Fullerton, where he has
taught since 1971. He received his S.T.B. and S.T.L.
degrees from the Marianum, Rome. He has a diploma in
Library Science from the Vatican Library and a Ph.D.
in religion and religious education from the Catholic
University of America. Besides Fullerton, he has
taught in Washington, Rome, Denver, and Los Angeles.
He has published articles in Bibliotheca Servorum
Yeneta, Communio, The Living Light, Marianum, Moniales
Ordinis Servorum, Studi Storici, Religion Teacher's
Journal, The Way, and Worship. He has also contributed
more than 25 reviews to magazines in this country and
in Europe. He was named Director of the Florence
campus for the California State University and College
System for 1982-83.

Nathan R. Kollar is professor of religious studies at
St. John Fisher College, Rochester, N.Y. He is former
chairman of Fisher's Religious Studies Department as
well as of The Church/Liturgy/Sacraments Area of The
Washington Theological Union. He received his doctor-
ate from Catholic University, Washington, D.C., and
has taught at the Washington Theological Coalition,
St. Thomas University, Fredericton, N.B., Canada;
University of Windsor, Canada; Loyola University,
Chicago; and the University of Rochester. He is

210

author of five books; Songs of Suffering: The Dimensions of Suffering (1982) is the most recent. He has also written over 100 articles and reviews in scholarly and popular journals. He was chairman of the Eastern International Region of the American Academy of Religion from 1978-79.

Robert Kress is associate professor of systematic theology at Catholic University in Washington, D.C. With degrees in education, philosophy, and theology, he has taught at Vincennes University, St. Meinrad College and Seminary in St. Meinrad, Indiana; St. Louis University in Missouri; Notre Dame University in Indiana; University of Evansville, Evansville, Indiana and Indiana University, Bloomington, Indiana. Fr. Kress is the author of five books and over 90 articles and reviews in scholarly and popular journals. His Whither Womankind: The Humanity of Women received the College Theology Society Book of the Year Award for 1975. He recently was elected to the Board of Directors of the College Theology Society (1981-84).